4/09

D0198324

Read Me a Rhyme in Spanish and English

Léame una rima en español e inglés

Rose Zertuche Treviño

American Library Association
Chicago   2009

Rose Zertuche Treviño is a consultant in the area of services for youth. She developed the first bilingual Born to Read program and has presented Born to Read workshops throughout the country. She is the editor of *The Pura Belpré Awards: Celebrating Latino Authors and Illustrators* (American Library Association, 2006).

While extensive effort has gone into ensuring the reliability of information appearing in this book, the publisher makes no warranty, express or implied, on the accuracy or reliability of the information, and does not assume and hereby disclaims any liability to any person for any loss or damage caused by errors or omissions in this publication.

Song lyrics for "La granja" (pp. 40–41) copyright ©1994, José-Luis Orozco, lyrics and musical arrangement; song lyrics for "Las ruedas del camión" (pp. 50–51), "La Tía Mónica" (pp. 71–72), and "Juanito" (pp. 72–73) copyright ©1997, José-Luis Orozco, lyrics and musical arrangement. All rights reserved. Used by permission of the author. www.joseluisorozco.com.

The paper used in this publication meets the minimum requirements of American National Standard for Information Sciences—Permanence of Paper for Printed Library Materials, ANSI Z39.48-1992. ∞

Library of Congress Cataloging-in-Publication Data
Treviño, Rose Zertuche.
    Read me a rhyme in Spanish and English / Rose Zertuche Treviño.
      p. cm.
    Includes bibliographical references and index.
    ISBN 978-0-8389-0982-9 (alk. paper)
    1. Children's libraries—Activity programs—United States.   2. Children's libraries—Services to Hispanic Americans.   3. Hispanic American children—Books and reading. 4. Children's songs, Spanish.   5. Children's literature, Spanish American—Bibliography.   6. Children's literature—Translations into Spanish—Bibliography. 7. Bilingual books—United States—Bibliography. I. Title.
    Z718.3T74 2009
    027.62'50973—dc22   2008045379

Copyright © 2009 by the American Library Association. All rights reserved except those which may be granted by Sections 107 and 108 of the Copyright Revision Act of 1976.

ISBN-13: 978-0-8389-0982-9

Printed in the United States of America
13 12 11 10 09   5 4 3 2 1

For my parents, Mary and Antonio Zertuche
Para mis padres, Maria y Antonio Zertuche

CONTENTS

ACKNOWLEDGMENTS

I have had the privilege of working with many of the finest children's librarians, and I would like to say thank you to those whom I have worked with who have also shared my passion for promoting bilingual services in the library. Thanks to all who read my manuscript and gave me much encouragement—Pete Treviño, Jaclyn Treviño Rendon, David Rendon, Margarita Zertuche, Gina Brudi, and Irene González; to Mary Zertuche, Nancy Bea Marchiori, and Vicky Valdez Treviño, who shared rhymes, songs, and tongue twisters and helped with some of the translations; and to Sonia Miller, who painstakingly read through the manuscript and checked for spelling, grammar, accent marks, tildes, and more. I am grateful to Steven Peter Treviño for drawing the craft patterns. I truly appreciate Luis Orozco and José-Luis Orozco, who have allowed me to use versions of some of the songs that the noted Mexican children's musician José-Luis Orozco has performed throughout the world and whose CD collections and book collections can be found in the discography and bibliography. And to Michael Jeffers, for all his work in making this book a reality.

INTRODUCTION

Open a book and a new adventure begins! Sharing the adventure gets better when you have an audience. Have you ever seen a baby's eyes widen when something special caught his or her eye? Have you ever seen a toddler jump for pure joy? Have you ever seen a child completely absorbed in something? These are all moments to enjoy, and for those of us who work with children, they can mean instant smiles. Programs for children are essential, and the world of books and reading should be available to all children regardless of their first language.

This book will give you ideas on programs for babies, toddlers, preschoolers, and school-age children for whom Spanish is the language spoken in the home. Books listed are either bilingual or available in separate English and Spanish editions. In some cases, only a Spanish version is available. The majority of nursery rhymes, lullabies, songs, and fingerplays are from Latin American countries and have been translated into English. You will not find Humpty Dumpty or Jack and Jill here, as there is no Mother Goose in Latin America. You will be introduced to Pimpón, La Feria de San Juan, and Doña Blanca. You'll feel the beat to chants of "tortillitas," "papas y papas," and much more.

Libraries are free for everyone, and those of us who work in libraries should make sure that our libraries welcome all, including new immigrants, folks for whom English is a second language, folks who do not speak English, people of color, people of all socioeconomic backgrounds, and even our tiniest customers. Although you won't find babies crawling to the library on their own, a wide range of programs, services, and materials will attract parents, who bring their children, check out books, attend our programs, and in doing so support libraries.

Invest in a child. It is one of the best investments you will make and our kids will be winners, as will all of us who support them.

Chapter 1

READING BEGINS AT HOME
EL GUSTO POR LEER COMIENZA EN LA CASA

All parents are their child's first teachers, but some parents do not understand that. As educators, we should be sending that message to every parent we encounter. In the Latino culture, a parent's role is as the nurturer. The mother is the loving, caring person who feeds the children, clothes them, and picks them up when they are hurt. The father is the person who provides for the family and who disciplines children. The role of teacher is left to the teacher in the school. This is slowly changing as more and more librarians seek opportunities to bring the message of first teacher to parents.

As a librarian working with the Born to Read program, I developed a simple list for parents that I translated into Spanish. This list follows, and you may want to tailor it for your library and for your customers. Whether the parent speaks Spanish or English, is Latino or not, the list is a good starting point as you promote your message that reading to a baby is important and that it is a good first step.

Reading tips for parents:

- Turn off the television and radio before you begin reading with your baby.
- Sit your baby on your lap or close to you on the floor.
- Read with emotion, and change your voice for different characters.
- Show your baby the pictures in the book.
- Set aside a special reading time each day.
- Let your baby be noisy and active while you are reading.

Consejos para cuando lees con tu bebé:

- Apaga la televisión y el radio antes de comenzar a leer con tu bebé.
- Sienta a tu bebé en tu regazo o junto a ti en el piso.
- Lee con emoción y cambia el tono de tu voz para los diferentes personajes del cuento.
- Muestra a tu bebé los dibujos en el libro.
- Reserva un tiempo especial para leer cada día.
- Deja a tu bebé que sea ruidoso y activo cuando lees.

This next list can also be used for parents of older children. You are also encouraged to develop bilingual fliers. Promoting your bilingual programs with a bilingual flier is the key to reaching many of the parents you need to reach. You may find a mixture of parents in your audience, including some who do not speak Spanish but want their children to learn Spanish. Always welcome your entire group.

Reading begins at home:

- Read to your children.
- Tell your children stories about your family.
- Limit the time your children spend watching television.
- Keep a collection of children's books and magazines at home.
- Sing to your children.
- Recite nursery rhymes to your children.
- Take your children to the library to check out books.
- Bring your children to storytime at the library.

El gusto por leer comienza en la casa:

- Lee junto con sus niños.
- Cuéntale a sus niños historias sobre la familia.
- Limita la cantidad de tiempo que sus niños pasan viendo televisión.
- Ten libros y revistas para los niños en la casa.
- Canta a sus niños.
- Comparte con sus niños sus rimas favoritas.
- Lleva a sus niños a la biblioteca y pida libros prestados para ellos.
- Lleva a sus niños a la hora en que se leen cuentos en la biblioteca.

PROMOTING THE LIBRARY

The ideas presented in this book are for the hard to reach. These are the people who are unaware of free library services and programs. Generally, you will find that more-educated Latino families are aware of such services and programs and do use the library. They know where to seek help and how to find libraries.

You will have to leave your library and visit your neighborhood to get a feel for where some Latino parents and their children can be found. Here are some places to visit:

- The grocery store
- The Laundromat
- Service organizations like the Women, Infants, and Children (WIC) clinic
- The Head Start center
- Churches
- Doctors' offices
- The flea market
- The *panadería* (bakery)
- Family restaurants like pizza places
- The mall
- Sports and recreation sites like the YMCA
- Schools
- Day-care centers

Your next step is to walk right in and introduce yourself. Ask to speak to the owner or manager. If he or she is unavailable, make an appointment. Develop a friendly business transaction and let the owner or manager know that your business is books and about the importance that reading plays in a child's success. Ask if you can promote your bilingual storytimes with a poster. Perhaps the owner or manager is willing to allow you to leave bookmarks. Be innovative and don't be afraid to ask. Some of these people may have children of their own.

Contact the churches in the neighborhood. Some churches print a weekly bulletin. You might be able to advertise your library and your bilingual storytime in the bulletin. While at the church, find out about the annual festival. Many churches hold one, and they are usually packed with families. Have a library booth at the festival where you can do simple crafts with children, talk about library services, and help families fill out library card applications. Be friendly and approachable, and sell the library!

Consider contacting the immigration center. Perhaps people there would be willing to insert a flier about library services into their welcome package for new immigrants. Be sure that the flier is bilingual. Although libraries are free in the United States, that is not the case in many countries. Another agency to contact is United Way, which works with many of the families you want to reach.

Visit management at the apartment complexes in your library's service area. Some complexes have a monthly one-page news flier. Your library could make the front page!

FORMING COMMUNITY PARTNERSHIPS

Form a partnership with the schools in your area. Offer to set up a table at back-to-school events. You can distribute your bilingual fliers there. Meet with the school librarian and join forces to promote neighborhood library services. Your school librarian will become invaluable. The school librarian has access to the very kids you want to reach. Some schools have a Head Start program in the building, so do some investigating. You may hit the jackpot!

If you do not ask for partners in your effort to reach your target audience, you will never know who might have jumped on board, so begin by making a list of people you can contact. Some additional suggestions to those listed previously include early childhood centers, bookstores, the state library, the Hispanic chamber of commerce, and retail stores. Approaching potential partners by phone or with a letter defining the library's bilingual storytimes and including the date, time, and location is a good first step. Tell them how you see them involved with promoting your program. If you write a letter or send an e-mail, include your contact information and a note explaining that you will follow up with a phone call if you do not hear back from them by a particular date.

Never underestimate the media. You will be surprised to see big numbers of people if you involve the media from the start. Contact and advertise in local newspapers, on radio and television stations, and with local businesses. Send a "fast facts" letter along with your invitation to jump on board to support literacy, increase the numbers of new readers, and engage in the success of children.

ESTABLISHING TRUST

Some people have misconceptions that Latinos do not use the library, that Latinos do not check out books, and that Latinos don't ask for help if they do come into the library.

Misconception #1: Latinos Do Not Use the Library

It is very important to establish trust with all customers. This is even more important with Latinos. There are several factors to consider. Some Latinos often see libraries as being for the educated, as costing money to use, or as being only for the elite. In many Latin American countries, there are no public libraries. Libraries are for research purposes, and one must pay to use the library. For many families, a library experience is not part of their background. The grandparents did not have a library, so this was not something that they would have passed on to their children. Those children, now adults, did not grow up with libraries, and the cycle is ready to continue. Unless those adults begin to understand how important books and reading are to their child's success, they may continue to pass up the opportunities at the library. This is where the librarian steps in and begins establishing trust, promoting library services, and developing programs of interest to Latinos.

Misconception #2: Latinos Do Not Check Out Books

Many libraries have a look about them that says "government entity." Signage that says "welcome" and "bienvenidos" will catch the attention of those whose preferred language is Spanish. The library card application should be simple and easy to fill out and should be available in Spanish and English. There should always be a welcome smile on the face of the first person a customer will encounter, and that person should make the effort to assist in any way possible, even helping fill out the library card application. Some Latinos may be immigrant families who fear the government. They may or may not be in the country legally, and they may or may not know someone who has entered the country illegally. Fear of immigration, or *la migra,* will prevent them from filling out a library card application because then they will be "on record." Keep your collection current and in good condition. Make sure it is visible. Weed regularly. Your Spanish-language collection should be just as important as any other collection in your library.

Misconception #3: Latinos Don't Ask for Help If They Do Come into the Library

Latinos generally do not want to put anyone out. Asking for help means interruption, and this is something that is difficult for some Latinos. Once again, there should always be a welcome smile on the face of the first person a customer will encounter when he or she enters the library, and that person should make the effort to assist in any way possible. Make an effort to approach customers as they enter the library. Welcome them and offer to help them find books, DVDs, the computer, and more. Be sure to take them to someone on staff who speaks Spanish if you are unable to communicate with them; however, that first welcoming effort is very important.

THE BOOKS

The books suggested here can be substituted for others, and at the end of each program idea there is a list of additional titles. For those of us who read to children, we understand how important it is to know and love the book. Examine each book carefully. Some of the suggested titles are board books and some have movable parts, such as flaps to lift and tabs to pull. If you do not particularly care for this type of book, don't use it. New books are always being published that you will want to examine as well. Review the bibliography for an annotation of each book. I have made every attempt to note when a book is a board book or has distinct features like movable parts. In some cases, I have suggested books written in Spanish by Latino authors that do not have English translations. Use your library collection to find similar books in English. You are the best judge as to which books from your English collection you will want to use during storytime.

THE RHYMES AND THE SONGS

I have included a separate discography listing resources that contain CD collections with many of the rhymes and songs you will find throughout this book. If you do not know the tunes, you may want to purchase the CDs and learn some of them. Another suggestion is to partner with a teacher or day-care provider who speaks Spanish and is familiar with many of these selections.

THE TRANSLATIONS

It is not an easy task to translate from one language to another. Some of the translations you will find within this book are not literal translations. You will also find that some do not make sense in English. They may also not make sense in Spanish, but they are traditional rhymes and songs loved and cherished by generations of children.

LATINO, HISPANIC, OR OTHER

For the purpose of continuity, I have used the term *Latino* to describe the customers who are of Latin American heritage. You will have to decide which term your community accepts. There are many countries that have been placed into this category and include people of different countries and regions, including Spain, Puerto Rico, Central America, South America, Mexico, the Caribbean, and more. If you serve a population from El Salvador, for example, they can help you determine how you can best promote services for this group. In parts of Texas, one might find a large percentage of people from Mexico. In New York, a large percentage might be Puerto Rican.

SOURCES

Many of the rhymes, songs, fingerplays, and tongue twisters included herein are well loved in Latin American countries. Some are part of oral tradition, and parents teach them to their children. Others I learned at library workshops and conference programs. I have made every attempt to find sources for those that may have appeared on a handout that I kept and used at countless storytimes throughout my career as a children's librarian. Some of the games and songs were those that my mother played as a child and taught me, while I learned some through my interaction with numerous agencies that serve Spanish-speaking children. Some I made up and have used with young children and are similar to those I learned. I contacted a few people for guidance regarding public domain and fair use. My intent is to provide those who work with children with a guide for planning and implementing a bilingual storytime. I wish you much success as you take a step toward storytimes in two languages.

Chapter 2

PROGRAMS FOR BABIES
PROGRAMAS PARA BEBÉS

B abies love to hear sounds and look at their surroundings, and they love to be the center of attention. An infant lap-sit program engages parent and baby to bond with books and to begin their library experience in a safe environment. Every baby deserves a good first start, and every proud parent will tell you that his or her baby is brilliant. They all are, and you can share in their brilliant development.

A bilingual program just for babies and their parents provides twice the fun and is the beginning of a learning time in two languages. You can make the most of this time by starting with a simple rhyme or song to be repeated in both languages. You will be the best judge as to which language to introduce first. You can also choose to start all of your bilingual story-times the same way. Repetition is very important for babies because they are beginning their language development. It is OK to repeat a rhyme several times or to read the same book several weeks in a row. If funds are available, multiple copies of the board books you will be sharing are best distributed to parents so that they and their baby can follow along with you.

Babies have a short attention span, so a simple program with plenty of variety lasting ten to fifteen minutes may be what you plan for.

After the stories, rhymes, songs, and fingerplays you can bring out a few toys for social time with babies.

It is always a good idea to have books within grasp just ready to be checked out. Place a few musical CDs on your table with the books, and make time to engage the parents by offering any one of the following:

- A bilingual handout listing the titles of the books you shared
- Words to the bilingual rhymes, songs, and fingerplays

- Suggested resources with additional ideas to use at home
- A schedule with your storytime listings

Looking for a name for your program? Here are a few ideas:

Cuentitos para bebés	Stories for Babies
Tiempo para bebés	Baby Time
Jardín de bebés	Baby Garden

Here is a very simple song that you can sing to the tune of "Frère Jacques." In Spanish, a song is called a *canción* or sometimes even a *cancioncita*, or "little song." *Bebé* with the accent on the second *e* means "baby." *Mami* is "mommy" and *papi* is "daddy."

HOLA, BEBÉ

Hola, bebé. Hola, bebé.
¿Cómo estás? ¿Cómo estás?
Muy bien, gracias.
   Muy bien, gracias.
¿Y usted? ¿Y usted?

Hola, mami. Hola, mami.
¿Cómo estás? ¿Cómo estás?
Muy bien, gracias.
   Muy bien, gracias.
¿Y usted? ¿Y usted?

Hola, papi. Hola, papi.
¿Cómo estás? ¿Cómo estás?
Muy bien, gracias.
   Muy bien, gracias.
¿Y usted? ¿Y usted?

HELLO, BABY

Hello, baby. Hello, baby.
How are you? How are you?
Very well, thank you.
   Very well, thank you.
How about you? How about you?

Hello, Mommy. Hello, Mommy.
How are you? How are you?
Very well, thank you.
   Very well, thank you.
How about you? How about you?

Hello, Daddy. Hello, Daddy.
How are you? How are you?
Very well, thank you.
   Very well, thank you.
How about you? How about you?

PROGRAM 1: THE ALPHABET / *EL ALFABETO*

This program introduces the alphabet to your group.

Opening Song

Sing the opening song, "Hola, bebé / Hello, Baby."

Book

Start with this simple book that is available in a bilingual edition in board-book format.

Rosa-Mendoza, Gladys. *The Alphabet / El alfabeto*. Me+mi, 2005.

Tickle Rhyme

Next, have parents try this tickle rhyme on baby's toes or fingers, with each toe being one of the vowels. For the second line, the parent runs his or her fingers up baby's leg to baby's belly button and then begins to tickle. In Spanish, a rhyme is called a *rima*.

A, E, I, O, U.   A, E, I, O, U.
El burro sabe más que tú.   The donkey knows more than you.

Once the parents try the rhyme on the right foot or hand, baby will be ready to try it out on the left. So try it again.

Book

Margarita Robleda is a well-known author and singer from Mexico who has written many books for young children. Here is one of her alphabet books.

Robleda, Margarita. *Jugando con las vocales*. Santillana USA, 2006.

Fingerplay

This silly fingerplay is a play on the vowels. You will notice that the burro is a character here, too. Start with the thumb and end with the pinkie. You can ask the parents to repeat after you as you start on one hand in Spanish and then on the other hand in English. In Spanish, a fingerplay is called a *juego con los dedos*.

A, el burro se va.   A, there goes the donkey.
E, el burro se fue.   E, there went the donkey.
I, el burro está aquí.   I, the donkey is here.
O, el burro se ahogó.   O, the donkey choked.
U, el burro eres tú.   U, you are the donkey.

Call-and-Response Rhyme

Next, try this simple rhyme as a call-and-response.

Las cinco vocales son	The five vowels are
A, E, I, O, U.	A, E, I, O, U.
A, E, I, O, U.	A, E, I, O, U.
Éstas son las cinco vocales.	These are the five vowels.

Book

Are you ready for another book? You will be the best person to know when to stop.

Salas, Michele. *A Is for Alphabet / A de alfabeto*. Everest, 2003.

Rhyme

Now try this final rhyme. It is a rhyme about the laughing vowels. You will notice that each line that follows the vowel is made to sound like the vowel, so that the *A* in Spanish sounds like "ah" and laughs "ha, ha, ha" and so forth. Here's a simple sound guide:

A in Spanish sounds like "ah."
E in Spanish sounds like "eh."
I in Spanish sounds like "ee."
O in Spanish sounds like "oh."
U in Spanish sounds like "ooh."

VOCALES	VOWELS
Así se ríe la A:	The A laughs like this:
Ja, ja, ja.	Ha, ha, ha.
Así se ríe la E:	The E laughs like this:
Je, je, je.	Heh, heh, heh.
Pero ríe más la I	But the I laughs longest
Porque se parece a mí:	Because it looks like me:
Ji, ji, ji.	Hee, hee, hee.
Así se ríe la O:	The O laughs like this:
Jo, jo, jo.	Ho, ho, ho.
Pero no ríe la U.	But the U doesn't laugh.
¿Por qué no ríe la U?	Why not?
Porque el burro sabe más	Because the donkey knows
que tú.	more than you.

Additional Books

Here are a few more alphabet books. The ones by Alberto Blanco, Marifé González, and Vicky Sempere are available only in Spanish. You might have these and other alphabet books for parents to choose from, and if you announce this before they leave, the books are sure to go with them.

Alvarez, Lourdes M. *Alphabet*. Sweetwater Press, 2005. Spanish: *Alfabeto*. Sweetwater Press, 2005.

Blanco, Alberto. *ABC*. Sistemas Técnicos de Edición, 2001.

González, Marifé. *Aprende las letras*. Susaeta, 2004.

Sempere, Vicky. *ABC*. Ediciones Ekaré, 1991.

Suárez, Maribel. *The Letters / Las letras*. Editorial Grijalbo, 1990.

Closing Song

Your program is now ending, so it is time for a closing tune. You can use the same tune you started with and just change a few words.

Adios, bebé. Adios, bebé.	Good-bye, baby. Good-bye, baby.
Ya te vas. Ya te vas.	Time to go. Time to go.
Con rimas y canciones,	With rhymes and songs,
Con rimas y canciones	With rhymes and songs,
Y cuentos también,	And stories too,
Y cuentos también.	And stories too.

PROGRAM 2: BABY ANIMALS / *LOS ANIMALITOS*

Opening Song

Welcome your babies and parents to your storytime with your welcome song, "Hola, bebé / Hello, Baby."

Vocabulary Activity

Next, introduce pictures of animals and make animal sounds. Make this a fun activity for baby and parent in two languages. Here are a few bilingual animals and what they sound like:

La vaca dice muu.	The cow says moo.
El perrito dice guau guau.	The puppy says bowwow.
El patito dice cuá, cuá.	The duckling says quack, quack.

La oveja dice behhh, behhh.	The sheep says baa, baa.
El pavo dice gluglú, gluglú.	The turkey says gobble, gobble.
El gallo dice kikirikí.	The rooster says cock-a-doodle-doo.

Book

Show your first book and start with the cover, introducing the title of the book, the author, and the illustrator. If you have a healthy budget or generous customers, you may be able to purchase plastic yellow ducks, one for each of your babies. This will be a take-home gift, as you know that the ducks will be in babies' mouths almost immediately. Be sure the ducks are big enough and don't have removable parts so that they don't pose a choking hazard.

This edition is a board book. It is available in separate English and Spanish editions and is about five little ducks that manage to get lost so that their mama has to go out and find them.

Paparone, Pamela. *Five Little Ducks*. North-South Books, 2005.
Spanish: *Los cinco patitos*. North-South Books, 2007.

Rhyme

Try this nonsense rhyme about a duck with eyes on the back of his head!

EL PATO	THE DUCK
Hay un pato bizco	There is a cross eyed duck
Que se cae cada rato;	Who always seems to fall;
¡Hombre!, pobre pato,	Well, poor duck,
¡Con los ojos al revés!	His eyes are on the back of his head!

Book

The next book to share, available in a bilingual edition, is about a kitten that never seems to come when called.

Mora, Pat. *Here, Kitty, Kitty! / ¡Ven, gatita, ven!* Rayo, 2008.

Rhyme

Here is a traditional rhyme. Encourage parents to gently bounce baby on their lap.

ARRE, BORRIQUITO
Arre, borriquito,
Vamos a Belén,
Que mañana es fiesta
Y al otro también.
Arre, arre, arre,
Anda más de prisa que
    llegamos tarde.

GIDDYUP, LITTLE BURRO
Giddyup, little burro,
We're off to Bethlehem.
Tomorrow is fiesta
And the next day too.
Giddyup, giddyup, giddyup,
Let's not be late.

Book

Try this big board book with your group. You might remember *Piggies* by Audrey Wood, and now the book is available in a perfect format for babies and toddlers.

Wood, Audrey. *Piggies / Cerditos: Lap-Sized Board Book*. Harcourt, 2008.

Fingerplay

Here is a fingerplay perfect for baby's toes or fingers.

LOS COCHINITOS
Éste compró un huevo.
Éste encendió el fuego.
Éste trajó la sal.
Éste lo cocinó
Y este pícaro gordo se lo
    comió.

THE LITTLE PIGS
This one bought an egg.
This one started the fire.
This one brought the salt.
This one cooked it,
And this naughty fat one
    ate it.

Clapping Rhyme

You can try one of these clapping rhymes:

PALMITAS
Palmitas, palmitas,
Que viene papá
Y trae un perrito
Que dice guau guau.

LET'S CLAP
Let's clap and clap,
Daddy's coming now.
He's bringing home a puppy
That says bowwow.

TILÍN, TILÍN
Tilín, tilín
Mi perro Pepín

TROT, TROT
Trot, trot
My dog Spot

Con orejas de trapo	With ears made of cloth
Y patas de serrín.	And paws made of straw.

Additional Books

Here are a few more books about animals that you can substitute or have available for parents to check out.

Inaraja, Javier. *El conejito volador.* Susaeta, 2005.

Mantoni, Elisa. *At school / En el colegio.* Everest, 2005.

Nava, Emanuela. *Una merienda de hielo.* Anaya, 2006.

Put, Klaartje van der. *El ratón Pimpón.* Bruño, 2006.

Rubio, Gabriela. *¿Dónde estoy?* Ediciones Ekaré, 2007.

Wildsmith, Brian. *Animal Colors / Los colores de los animales.* Star Bright Books, 2005.

Closing Song

You can choose to end your program with the "Adios, bebé / Good-bye, Baby" song or find one that you are most comfortable with. You might even want to close with the song "Los pollitos / Baby Chicks." You can use arm and finger motions to play out the parts, and include rocking baby at the end with a final big hug.

LOS POLLITOS	BABY CHICKS
Los pollitos dicen	Baby chicks are singing
Pío, pío, pío,	Peep, peep, peep,
Cuando tienen hambre,	Every time they're hungry,
Cuando tienen frío.	Every time they're cold.
La gallina busca	Mama looks for wheat,
El maíz y el trigo,	Then she looks for corn,
Les da la comida	Then she feeds them dinner,
Y les presta abrigo.	And she keeps them warm.
Bajo sus dos alas,	Under Mama's wings,
Acurrucaditos,	Sleeping in the hay,
Duermen los pollitos,	Sleeping baby chicks,
Hasta el otro día.	Until the next day.

PROGRAM 3: BABIES / *LOS BEBÉS*

Have you ever noticed that babies love other babies? They reach out to one another. Books about babies will be fun to share.

Opening Activity

Start your program with your welcome song, welcome rhyme, or welcome fingerplay. You decide. It's your program, and you need to feel comfortable and love what you are doing.

Fingerplay

For this traditional fingerplay, start with the baby's thumb or big toe. Go from thumb to pinkie and then hug baby.

Este chiquito es mi hermanito	This tiny one is my little brother.
Ésta es mi mamá.	This one is my mother.
Este altito es mi papá.	This tall one is my father.
Ésta es mi hermana.	This one is my sister.
¡Y este chiquito y bonito soy yo!	And this little pretty one is me!

Book

This first book is a wordless book that shows a baby opposite a picture of an animal in a similar position or with a similar look. It is sure to bring laughs from the parents! Although wordless, you can fill in with words in Spanish and then in English. Ask the parents to join in as well.

Ceelen, Vicky. *Baby! Baby!* Random House, 2008.

Rhyme

This nursery rhyme is a favorite with babies. Ask parents to hold baby's hand open and tap baby's palm as the simple verse is recited.

Pon, pon, tata,	Pon, pon, la, la,
Mediecito pa' la papa;	A little sock from papa;
Pon, pon, tía,	Pon, pon, maybe,
Mediecito pa' sandía;	A little sock for baby;
Pon, pon, pon,	Pon, pon, pon,

Mediecito pa' jabón	Wash my socks
Y me lavan mi camisón.	And my nightie.

Book

A baby's belly button brings plenty of opportunities for peekaboo or for tickles. Try this book with your group of babies and try out all the actions, encouraging parents to play peekaboo with their babies as they look for baby's eyes, feet, and of course their belly button.

> Katz, Karen. *Where Is Baby's Belly Button?* Simon and Schuster Children's Publishing, 2000. Spanish: *¿Dónde está el ombliguito?* Simon and Schuster Libros para Niños, 2004.

Song

This following song has repetition, and baby can slowly bounce on a parent's lap to the tune of the song. There are several musical versions; you can go to the discography to look for Spanish music CDs for children.

Debajo de un botón-tón-tón,	Underneath a button-ton-ton,
Del Señor Martín-tín-tín,	Belonging to Martin-tin-tin,
Había un ratón-tón-tón,	There lived a little mouse-ouse-ouse,
Ay, ¡qué chiquitín-tín-tín!	Oh, how chiquitín-tín-tín!

Tickle Rhyme

Here is a tickle rhyme. Parents make walking motions with fingers on baby's arm. End at baby's belly button and begin to tickle.

Tú padre ha venido.	Here comes Daddy.
¿Y que me ha traido?	What did he bring me?
Un vestido.	A dress.
¿De qué color?	What color?
De cosquillas alrededor.	With tickles all around.

Book

All babies are beautiful and they love to be hugged and kissed. Here is a book available in Spanish and English all about babies and hugs and kisses.

> Intrater, Roberta Grobel. *Hugs and Kisses.* Scholastic, 2002. Spanish: *Besitos y abrazos.* Scholastic, 2002.

Motion Rhyme

Try this motion rhyme. Parents should rock baby on their laps back and forth. Take baby's hands and form a sun and then a moon. Next, make twinkling motions with your hands opening and closing rapidly.

EL DÍA EN QUE TÚ NACISTE	ON THE DAY YOU WERE BORN
El día en que tú naciste	On the day you were born
Nacieron las cosas bellas.	Beautiful things were born.
Nació el sol,	The sun,
Nació la luna,	The moon,
Nacieron las estrellas.	And the stars.

Additional Books

The following titles are books about babies and can be easily substituted with others. The first two titles below are available in Spanish only. The books by Elya and Wheeler are not bilingual but have Spanish words throughout.

Ashbé, Jeanne. *¡Eso no se hace!* Editorial Corimbo, 2001.

Carrier, Isabelle. *¿Un pequeño qué?* Edelvives, 2003.

Elya, Susan Middleton. *Bebé Goes Shopping.* Harcourt, 2006.

Sirett, Dawn. *Baby's Busy World.* DK Publishing, 2005. Spanish: *Bebés atareados.* Molino, 2006.

Suen, Anastasia. *Baby Born.* Lee and Low Books, 2000. Spanish: *Recién nacido.* Lee and Low Books, 2000.

Wheeler, Lisa. *Te amo, Bebé, Little One.* Little, Brown, 2004.

Closing Activity

End your program with your good-bye song or rhyme.

PROGRAM 4: FOOD / *LA COMIDA*

In preparation for this program, bring a few seasonal fruits and vegetables. Place them on a table and have small stand-up signs with the names of the fruits and vegetables in Spanish and in English.

Opening Activity

Begin your program with your welcome song or rhyme.

Vocabulary Activity

Draw attention to the fruits and vegetables and say the names with the parents as you hold up the item. These will one day be a part of the baby's vocabulary. Here are just a few fruits and vegetables, and you may want to ask the parents for suggestions:

la manzana	apple
el plátano	banana
el durazno	peach
la ciruela	plum
el pepino	cucumber
la papa	potato
los ejotes	string beans
la lechuga	lettuce

Book

Next, read the following book, which is part of a series published by Rayo, an imprint of HarperCollins.

Mora, Pat. *Let's Eat! / ¡A comer!* Rayo, 2008.

Clapping Rhyme

Here is a clapping rhyme about potatoes. You can try it as a call-and-response and encourage parents to hold baby's hands and clap with them.

PAPAS	POTATOES
Papas y papas para papá.	Potatoes, potatoes for Daddy.
Papas y papas para mamá.	Potatoes, potatoes for Mommy.
Las calientitas para papá.	The nice little hot ones for Daddy.
Las quemaditas para mamá.	The burnt little toasted ones for Mommy.

Now try it again and this time, give Mamá a chance for the nice little hot ones.

Papas y papas para mamá.	Potatoes, potatoes for Mommy.
Papas y papas para papá.	Potatoes, potatoes for Daddy.
Las calientitas para mamá.	The nice little hot ones for Mommy.
Las quemaditas para papá.	The burnt little toasted ones for Daddy.

Book

Follow up with this book available in Spanish and in English:

> Intrater, Roberta Grobel. *Eat!* Scholastic, 2002. Spanish: *¡Qué rico!* Scholastic, 2002.

Rhyme

Ask parents to bounce baby gently and recite this rhyme.

SEÑORA SANTA ANA	MRS. SANTA ANA
Señora Santa Ana,	Mrs. Santa Ana,
¿Por qué llora el niño?	why does the baby cry?
Por una manzana	Because of the apple
Que se le ha perdido.	That he cannot find.
Vamos a la huerta.	Let's go to the orchard.
Cortaremos dos.	There we will pick two.
Una para el niño,	One will be for baby,
Otra para Dios.	One will be for God.

Book

This book is available only in Spanish. Ana Cristina wants a cookie, and a surprise awaits her. After you read the story in Spanish, you can retell it in English. You can even ask parents to join in and help tell the story.

> Robleda, Margarita. *Una sorpresa para Ana Cristina*. Sitesa, 1992.

Rhyme

LERO, LERO, CANDELERO	MAKER, MAKER, CANDLEMAKER
Lero, lero, candelero,	Maker, maker, candlemaker,
Aquí te espero	Here I'll wait
Comiendo huevo	Eating an egg
Con la cuchara del cocinero.	With the cook's spoon.

Additional Books

These two books are available only in Spanish. Look for other titles in English.

Díaz-Toledo, Alonso. *¡A desayunar!* Susaeta, 2005.

Nava, Emanuela. *Una comida sorpresa.* Anaya, 2006.

Closing Activity

End with your good-bye song or rhyme.

PROGRAM 5: SHAPES / *LAS FORMAS*

Opening Activity

Begin with an opening song or rhyme.

Motion Rhyme

After your welcome song or rhyme, try this motion rhyme. Encourage parents to make the motions with their babies.

LAS MANITAS	LITTLE HANDS
Abrir y cerrar, abrir y cerrar.	Open and shut, open and shut.
Las manos al compás.	Do your hands like this.
Abrir y cerrar, abrir y cerrar.	Open and shut, open and shut.
Las manos hacia atrás.	Now put them behind you.
Suben, suben, suben,	Up, up, up,
Por el cielo así,	Higher up to the sky
Y cuando llegan a lo alto	And when they can climb no higher
Dan una palmada así.	They give a little clap.

Vocabulary Activity

In preparation for this program, you may want to have an assortment of colorful shapes. Hold one up at a time and call out the shapes in Spanish and then in English. Then, share this first book about shapes, which is available in Spanish and English.

el círculo	circle
el triángulo	triangle
el rectángulo	rectangle
el cuadrado	square

Book

Gunzi, Christiane. *My Very First Look at Shapes*. Two-Can Publishing, 2006. Spanish: *Mi primera mirada a las formas*. Two-Can Publishing, 2004.

Song

Here is a song to sing.

CABEZA, HOMBROS, PIERNAS Y PIES	HEAD, SHOULDERS, KNEES, AND TOES
Cabeza, hombros, piernas y pies,	Head, shoulders, knees, and toes,
Piernas y pies.	Knees and toes.
Cabeza, hombros, piernas y pies,	Head, shoulders, knees, and toes,
Piernas y pies.	Knees and toes.
Ojos, orejas, boca y nariz,	Eyes, ears, mouth, and nose,
Cabeza, hombros, piernas y pies,	Head, shoulders, knees, and toes,
Piernas y pies.	Knees and toes.

Additional Books

Another book to share might include any of the following:

Alvarez, Lourdes M. *Shapes*. Sweetwater Press, 2005. Spanish: *Formas*. Sweetwater Press, 2005.

Carril, Isabel. *Descubro las formas*. Bruño, 2007.

Emberly, Rebecca. *My Shapes / Mis formas*. Little, Brown, 2000.

Gaetán, Maura. *¿Qué forma tiene? Un libro sobre formas*. Editorial Sigmar, 2006.

Suárez, Maribel. *Las formas*. Sagebrush Education Resources, 1999.

Rhyme

Try this traditional rhyme slowly at first. Then try it again just a little bit faster, and one more time even faster.

TENGO MANITA	HERE IS MY HAND
Tengo manita.	Here is my hand.
No tengo manita,	Now it is hiding
Porque la tengo	Because it's now
Desconchabadita.	Completely behind me.

Closing Activity

End your program with your good-bye song or rhyme.

PROGRAM 6: FAMILY / *LA FAMILIA*

In many Latino families, grandparents live with their children and grandchildren. It is not at all uncommon for the oldest child, often the oldest daughter, to take on the responsibility of caring for aging parents.

Opening Activity

Begin with your welcome song or rhyme.

Vocabulary Activity

Next, talk about family members and identify them in Spanish and English. Here's a short list:

la mamá or mami	mama or mommy
el papá or papi	papa or daddy
el hermano	brother
el hermanito	little brother
la hermana	sister
la hermanita	little sister
la abuela, abuelita, or nana	grandma
el abuelo or abuelito	grandpa

Book

Start with this book about a little boy who goes from room to room looking for his mommy.

Ramos, Mario. *Mommy! / ¡Mamá!* Corimbo, 2007.

Fingerplay

Here is a fingerplay. Start with the thumb. On the last line, ask parents to close baby's hand and kiss baby's fingers.

Mi mamá, toda cariño,	My loving mother,
Mi papá, todo bondad,	My good father,
Nuestro encanto, el dulce niño,	Our sweet, charming baby,
Mi hermanito alto y formal,	My tall and formal brother,
Y yo, en la casa, aliño.	And me, at home sitting pretty.
Vivimos en nuestro hogar.	We live together in our house.

Book

This very simple book can be shared next.

> Guy, Ginger Foglesong. *My Grandma / Mi abuelita*. HarperCollins, 2007.

Fingerplay

Another fingerplay to use on baby's fingers and toes is this simple one:

LA FAMILIA	THE FAMILY
Ésta es mamá.	This is mama.
Éste es papá.	This is papa.
Éste es hermano alto.	This is tall brother.
Éste es hermana.	This is sister.
Éste es bebé.	This is baby.
Y los queremos todos.	We love one another very much.

Book

If your audience of babies seems ready for another story, here is one to share.

> Roth, Susan L. *My Love for You / Mi amor por ti*. Dial, 2003.

Rhyme

You can recite this rhyme next. Bring along a clock.

EL RELOJ	THE CLOCK
El reloj de abuelo suena tic toc, tic toc.	Grandpa's clock goes ticktock, ticktock.
El reloj de mamá suena tic toc, tic toc.	Mama's clock goes ticktock, ticktock.
El relojito del niñito suena tic toc, tic toc,	Baby's little clock goes ticktock, ticktock,
Tic toc, tic toc, tic toc, tic toc, tic toc.	Ticktock, ticktock, ticktock, ticktock.

Additional Books

You might have an assortment of books on hand, including these:

> *All about baby / Todo sobre bebé*. DK Publishing, 2004.
>
> Beaton, Clare. *Family / La familia*. Barron's, 1997.

Gomi, Taro. *My friends / Mis amigos.* Chronicle Books, 2006.

Pérez, Amada Irma. *Nana's Big Surprise / Nana, ¡qué sorpresa!* Children's Book Press, 2007.

Rosa-Mendoza, Gladys. *What Time Is It? / ¿Qué hora es?* Me+mi, 2005.

Closing Activity

End your program with your good-bye song or rhyme.

PROGRAM 7: NUMBERS / *LOS NÚMEROS*

Along with colors and the alphabet, introduce numbers early. Babies are always ready to learn.

Opening Activity

Start your program with your opening song or rhyme.

Vocabulary Activity

You can begin counting with your group, and encourage parents to count from one to ten on baby's fingers and toes in Spanish and in English.

uno	one
dos	two
tres	three
cuatro	four
cinco	five
seis	six
siete	seven
ocho	eight
nueve	nine
diez	ten

Book

Next, share this book, which is available in Spanish and in English. Take time with each page and point to each number.

Alvarez, Lourdes M. *Numbers.* Sweetwater Press, 2005. Spanish: *Números.* Sweetwater Press, 2005.

Rhyme

Recite either or both of these traditional rhymes.

CINCO POLLITOS	**FIVE BABY CHICKS**
Cinco pollitos	My aunt has
Tiene mi tía.	Five baby chicks.
Uno le salta,	One jumps,
Otro le pía	One peeps,
Y tres le cantan	And three sing
La sinfonía.	A chorus.
LA GALLINA	**THE HEN**
La gallina popujada	The fat little hen
Puso un huevo en la cebada.	Laid an egg in the barley field.
Puso uno, puso dos,	One, two,
Puso tres, puso cuatro,	Three, four,
Puso cinco, puso seis,	Five, six,
Puso siete, puso ocho.	Seven, eight.

Book

You can share this book:

Cruz, Jimena. *Primeras palabras*. Editorial Sigmar, 2007.

Tickle Rhyme

This tickle rhyme has the parent counting on baby's toes or baby's fingers. Count from one to nine and begin tickling on the word *pingüino*.

PIN-UNO, PIN-DOS	**PEN-ONE, PEN-TWO**
Pin-uno, pin-dos, pin-tres,	Pen-one, pen-two, pen-three,
Pin-cuatro, pin-cinco, pin-seis,	Pen-four, pen-five, pen-six,
Pin-siete, pin-ocho, pin-nueve,	Pen-seven, pen-eight, pen-nine,
Pingüino.	Penguin.

Book

Here is a simple book on numbers available in Spanish and in English:

Gunzi, Christiane. *My Very First Look at Numbers*. Two-Can Publishing, 2006. Spanish: *Mi primera mirada a los números*. Two-Can Publishing, 2004.

Rhyme

Pinocchio can be found in many Latin rhymes. He is a character for babies to meet. In this one, Pinocchio wants you to count from one to eight. Ask parents to count off the numbers on baby's hands or toes.

CALLE DEL OCHO	EIGHTH STREET
En la calle del ocho	On Eighth Street
Me encontré a Pinocho,	I met Pinocchio,
Y me dijó que contará	And he asked me to count
Del uno al ocho:	from one to eight:
Uno, dos, tres, cuatro, cinco,	One, two, three, four, five,
Seis, siete, ocho.	Six, seven, eight.

Additional Books

These are a few more suggested titles:

Baker, Alan. *Little Rabbits' First Number Book*. Kingfisher, 1998. Spanish: *Los números*. Kingfisher, 2003.

Dodd, Emma. *123 Lolo: Un cuento sobre números y colores*. Random House, 2004.

Grez, M. *Contamos 10 en el mar*. Susaeta, 2005.

Sempere, Vicky. *1, 2, 3: Un cuento para contar*. Ediciones Ekaré, 1995.

Closing Activity

End your program with your good-bye song or rhyme.

PROGRAM 8: DREAMS AND LULLABIES / *SUEÑOS Y ARRULLOS*

You can offer a bedtime story program for your babies, and ask parents to bring babies in their pajamas with a favorite stuffed animal.

Opening Activity

Begin with your opening song or rhyme and then share a book.

Book

Brown, Margaret Wise. *Goodnight Moon 1, 2, 3: A Counting Book / Buenas noches, luna, 1, 2, 3: Un libro para contar*. Rayo, 2007.

Tickle Rhyme

Here is a tickle rhyme. Be sure to have parents tickle babies on their tummies on the last line:

LA LUNA	THE MOON
Aquí viene la luna,	Here comes the moon,
Comiendo tuna,	Eating prickly-pear fruit,
Echando cáscaras en la laguna.	Throwing peels into the pond.

Book

Try this sweet story by the award-winning author and poet Pat Mora:

Mora, Pat. *Sweet Dreams / Dulces sueños*. Rayo, 2008.

Song

Sing this traditional Latin American song using hand motions with baby. Parents can pretend that their child is Pimpón and can make the motions with baby of washing hands and face, combing hair, and so forth.

PIMPÓN	PIMPÓN
Pimpón es un muñeco	Pimpón is a doll,
Muy guapo de cartón.	A handsome cardboard doll.
Se lava sus manitas	He washes his little hands
Con agua y con jabón.	With water and with soap.
Pimpón es un muñeco	Pimpón is a doll,
Muy guapo de cartón.	A handsome cardboard doll.
Se lava la carita	He washes his face
Con agua y con jabón.	With water and with soap.
Se peina con un peine	He combs his hair with a comb,
Muy duro de marfil.	A strong comb made of ivory.
Y aunque no le gusta,	And though he doesn't like it,
No llora, ni hace así.	He doesn't cry like this.
Pimpón me da la mano	Pimpón shakes hands with me
Con un fuerte apretón,	With a very strong squeeze.
Que quiero ser tu amigo	He wants to be my friend,
Pimpón, Pimpón, Pimpón.	Pimpón, Pimpón, Pimpón.

Apenas las estrellas	And when the stars
Empiezan a salir,	Begin to shine,
Pimpón se va a la cama.	Pimpón then goes to bed.
Pimpón se va a dormir.	Pimpón then goes to sleep.

Book

Next, read this story:

> Morales, Yuyi. *Little Night*. Roaring Brook Press, 2007. Spanish: *Nochecita*. Roaring Brook Press, 2007.

Song

Ask parents to rock their babies while you sing this lullaby:

A LA RORRO	**ROCK-A-BYE**
A la rorrororro niño,	Rock-a-bye, baby,
A la rorro rorro ro	Rock-a-bye;
Duérmete, mi niño,	Sleep, my baby,
Duérmete, mi amor.	Sleep, my love.
Tus ojitos bailan	Your eyes are twinkling
Cual la luz del sol;	Like the bright little sun;
Duérmete, mi niño,	Sleep, my child,
Duérmete, mi amor.	Sleep, my love.

Rhyme

Ask parents to sit baby on their lap facing them and to repeat this traditional lullaby rhyme to a steady rhythm with you:

ESTE NIÑO TIENE SUEÑO	**THIS CHILD IS SLEEPY**
Este niño tiene sueño.	This child is sleepy.
Tiene ganas de dormir.	He wants to go to bed.
Tiene un ojito cerrado	He has one eye closed
Y otro no lo puede abrir.	And can't seem to open the other.

Additional Books

These are a few other books to use:

> Díaz-Toledo, Alonso. *¡A dormir!* Susaeta, 2005.
>
> Intrater, Roberta Grobel. *Sleepyheads*. Scholastic, 2002. Spanish: *Dulces sueños*. Scholastic, 2002.

Nava, Emanuela. *Arrullos y caricias*. Anaya, 2006.

Peek, Merle. *Roll Over! A Counting Song / ¡Dénse vuelta! Una canción de cuentos*. Clarion Books, 2008.

Robleda, Margarita. *Dreams*. Santillana USA, 2004. Spanish: *Sueños*. Santillana USA, 2004.

Weeks, Sarah. *Counting Ovejas*. Atheneum Books for Young Readers, 2006.

Closing Activity

End your program with your good-bye song or rhyme.

Chapter 3

PROGRAMS FOR TODDLERS
PROGRAMAS PARA NIÑOS PEQUEÑOS

Sitting still is not what toddlers are made of, as their attention span is short, so be prepared for wiggling, wandering children who may decide to sit on your lap as you proceed to read a book. Toddlers are exploring their world, and everything belongs to them. They haven't yet learned to share, so a little trauma during storytime might occur if you bring out the musical instruments or the toys. The key to storytime for this age group includes variety with songs, fingerplays, and nursery rhymes mixed in between stories. Select books with large, colorful pictures and minimal text. Be ready for interruptions. You should plan for the program to last between fifteen and twenty minutes for this group.

A bilingual program for children gives you an opportunity to have fun with these inquisitive minds. At this stage, toddlers can clap their hands, stomp their feet, jump, and even run from you. They learn fast and will soon be counting with you in two languages. Start your toddler program with a song or a rhyme that becomes something familiar to them that they will always connect with the library.

Here's one you might want to try:

PULGARCITO	WHERE IS THUMBKIN?
Pulgarcito.	Where is thumbkin?
Pulgarcito.	Where is thumbkin?
¿Dónde estás?	Where are you?
Aquí estoy.	Here I am.
Quiero saludarte.	Here I come to greet you.
Quiero saludarte.	Here I come to greet you.
Yo también.	Run and hide.
Yo también.	Run and hide.

It is always a good idea to have books within grasp just ready to be checked out. Place a few musical CDs on your table with the books and make time to engage the parents by offering any one of the following:

- A bilingual handout listing the titles of the books you shared
- Words to the bilingual rhymes, songs, and fingerplays
- Suggested resources with additional ideas to use at home
- A schedule with your storytime listings

Get your toddler group and their parents used to your program, and give it an engaging name like one of the following:

Jardín de cuentos	Story Garden
Cuentitos, rimas y más	Stories, Rhymes, and More
Jardín Infantil	Children's Garden

PROGRAM 1: ABC / 123

Opening Rhyme

Begin your program with your welcome rhyme in Spanish and English. Invite parents to participate with their children.

Book

Here's a book to start with about some animal friends on their way to surprise Zelda the zebra on her birthday:

Miranda, Anne. *Alphabet Fiesta: An English/Spanish Alphabet Story.* Turtle Books, 2001.

Clapping Rhyme

Now try this traditional clapping rhyme about chocolate. *Chocolate* is spelled the same in Spanish but instead of two syllables, there are four. Clap your hands to a steady rhythm and do a call-and-response with this song. You can purchase a *molinillo,* which is a Mexican kitchen tool for whipping chocolate. It is a long stick, and you dip the larger circular end into the pot and rub your hands together with the top part between your two hands.

EL CHOCOLATE	CHOCOLATE
Uno, dos, tres, CHO	One, two, three, CHO
Uno, dos, tres, CO	One, two, three, CO

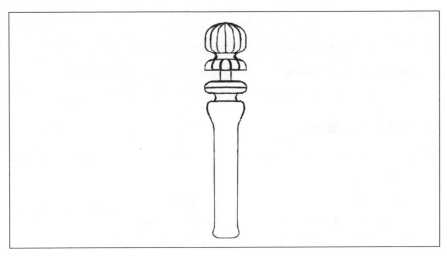

Molinillo

Uno, dos, tres, LA
Uno, dos, tres, TE

One, two, three, LA
One, two, three, TE

Chocolate, chocolate,
Bate, bate chocolate.

Chocolate, chocolate,
Beat and beat the chocolate.

Book

Here is a bilingual ABC book featuring animals that introduce the different letters of the alphabet:

Coutinhas, João. *Animals from A to Z / Animales de la A a la Z.* Everest, 2003.

Rhyme

Next, try this number rhyme:

CUÉNTAME DIEZ
Los perros aquí,
Los gatos allá.
Cuéntame diez
Y yo me saldré.
Uno, dos, tres, cuatro, cinco,
Seis, siete, ocho, nueve y diez.

COUNT TO TEN
The dogs over here,
The cats over there.
Count to ten
And then I'll leave.
One, two, three, four, five,
Six, seven, eight, nine, and ten.

Book

The following book is available in a bilingual edition:

> Brusca, María Cristina. *Three Friends: A Counting Book / Tres amigos: Un cuento para contar.* Henry Holt, 1995.

Call-and-Response Rhyme

Ask parents to hold their toddler's hands and make the motions as you recite this call-and-response rhyme.

LOS DEDITOS	MY FINGERS
Tengo diez deditos.	I have ten fingers.
Diez deditos tengo yo.	Ten fingers have I.
Cuéntalos conmigo.	Count them out with me.
Uno, dos, tres,	One, two, three,
Cuatro, cinco, seis,	Four, five, six,
Siete, ocho, nueve,	Seven, eight, nine,
Y uno más son diez.	And one more makes ten.
Ya cuéntalos al revés	Now count them backward.
Diez, nueve, ocho,	Ten, nine, eight,
Siete, seis, cinco,	seven, six, five,
Cuatro, tres, dos, uno.	Four, three, two, one.
Diez deditos tengo yo.	Ten fingers have I.
Tengo diez deditos.	I have ten fingers.

Additional Books

Here is a list of titles that you can have available for parents to check out:

> Aigner-Clark, Julie. *Asómate y ve los números.* Advanced Marketing, 2003.
>
> Mora, Pat. *¡Marimba! Animales from A to Z.* Clarion Books, 2006.
>
> Mora, Pat. *Uno, dos, tres: 1, 2, 3.* Clarion, 1996.
>
> Palomar de Miguel, Juan. *Mis primeras letras de palabras mexicanas.* Ediciones Destino, 2004.
>
> Robleda, Margarita. *Mis letras favoritas.* Ediciones Destino, 2003.
>
> Suárez, Maribel. *¿Cuántos son?* Editorial Grijalbo, 1992.
>
> Walsh, Ellen Stoll. *Mouse Count.* Harcourt Children's Books, 1995. Spanish: *Cuenta ratones.* Fondo de Cultura Económica, 2003.

Closing Rhyme

End the program with the following rhyme:

Colorín, colorado,	*Colorín, colorado,*
Este cuento se ha acabado	This story is now over

Or you can change some of the words, like this:

Colorín, colorado,	*Colorín, colorado,*
Este programa se ha acabado	This program is now over.

Be sure to send home a flier with the titles of the books you read, the words to the songs and rhymes, and a list of reading tips.

PROGRAM 2: WATER / *EL AGUA*

You may want to purchase a small portable fountain that lets you add water to flow over rocks. This might intrigue your toddlers. They can each take a turn and investigate. Use your imagination and try something new. Perhaps you have the budget to purchase a case of bottled water in small toddler-size bottles that you can hand out with rules about drinking water in the library as they are leaving.

Opening Rhyme

Begin your program with your welcome rhyme in Spanish and English. Invite parents to participate with their children.

Book

Start with this book, which is available in Spanish and English and is based on a true story about ten rubber ducks that are scattered in different directions during a storm.

> Carle, Eric. *10 Little Rubber Ducks*. HarperCollins, 2005. Spanish: *10 patitos de goma*. Rayo, 2007.

Motion Rhyme

Next, recite this traditional rhyme and be sure to encourage your toddlers to make swimming motions.

NADABAN	SWIMMING
Nadaban y nadaban,	Swimming and swimming,
Nadaban los patitos.	The ducklings go by.
Nadaban y nadaban,	Swimming and swimming,
Y no se mojaban.	They always stay dry.

Book

Follow with this story:

Cruz, Jimena. *¡A nadar, pececito!* Editorial Sigmar, 2007.

Motion Rhyme

Now, engage your group in this motion rhyme about fish that swim and fish that fly. Ask your toddlers to pretend that they are the little fish as they act out the swimming and flying motions.

LOS PECECITOS	THE LITTLE FISH
Los pececitos nadan en el agua.	The little fish swim in the water.
Nadan, nadan, nadan.	They swim, swim, swim.
Vuelan, vuelan, vuelan.	They fly, fly, fly.
Son chiquititos, chiquititos.	They are tiny, tiny, tiny.
Vuelan, vuelan, vuelan.	Fly, fly, fly.
Nadan, nadan, nadan.	Swim, swim, swim.

Book

This bilingual story is about the ocean:

Ryan, Pam Muñoz. *Hello, Ocean / Hola, mar.* Charlesbridge, 2003.

Song

You can follow this up with a song about a little boat:

EL BARQUITO	THE LITTLE BOAT
Había una vez un barquito chiquitito,	There was once a small boat,
Había una vez un barquito chiquitito,	There was once a small boat,
Había una vez un barquito chiquitito,	There was once a small boat,
Y no podía, no podía, no podía navegar.	That just couldn't navigate.

Pasaron una, dos, tres, cuatro, cinco,	One, two, three, four, five,
Seis, siete semanas.	Six, seven weeks went by.
Pasaron una, dos, tres, cuatro, cinco,	One, two, three, four, five,
Seis, siete semanas.	Six, seven weeks went by.
Pasaron una, dos, tres, cuatro, cinco,	One, two, three, four, five,
Seis, siete semanas	Six, seven weeks went by.
Y el barquito, el barquito,	And the little boat, the little boat
No podía navegar,	Couldn't navigate
Y si la historia no les parece larga,	And if this story doesn't seem long
Y si la historia no les parece larga,	And if this story doesn't seem long
Y si la historia no les parece larga,	And if this story doesn't seem long
Volveremos, volveremos,	We can start, we can start
Volveremos a empezar.	We can start at the beginning again.

Additional Books

Here are some titles of books you can have for parents to check out after your program:

Cruz, Jimena. *Animales del mar.* Editorial Sigmar, 2007.

Intrater, Roberta Grobel. *Splish, Splash.* Scholastic, 2002. Spanish: ¡*Al agua, patos!* Scholastic, 2002.

Marzollo, Jean. *I Am Water.* Scholastic, 1996. Spanish: *Soy el agua.* Scholastic, 1999.

Mora, Pat. *Agua, agua, agua.* Scott, Foresman, 1995.

Nava, Emanuela. *Gotas y goterones.* Anaya, 2006.

Closing Rhyme

End your program with a closing rhyme or song. Be sure to send home a flier with the titles of the books you read, the words to the songs and rhymes, and a list of reading tips.

PROGRAM 3: COLORS / *LOS COLORES*

Opening Rhyme

Begin your program with your welcome rhyme in Spanish and English. Invite parents to participate with their children.

Book

Here's a book illustrated by the Caldecott Award–winning illustrator David Diaz with the words to the traditional song "De colores":

> *Bright with Colors / De colores*. Marshall Cavendish, 2008.

Rhyme

Recite this traditional rhyme:

Pito, pito,	Whistle, whistle
Colorito:	Many colors:
¿Dónde vas	Where are you going,
Tan bonito?	Pretty one?

Book

Next, share this book, available in Spanish and in English:

> Alvarez, Lourdes M. *Colors*. Sweetwater Press, 2004. Spanish: *Colores*. Sweetwater Press, 2004.

Fingerplay

Try this fingerplay and start with the pinkie. Point to one finger at a time. After you recite the last line, hide toddler's thumb behind his or her back.

El amarillo es mío.	Yellow is mine.
El rojo, tan flojo.	Red is lazy.
El blanco va al banco.	White goes to the bank.
El anaranjado está mojado.	Orange is all wet.
El verde se pierde.	Green gets lost.

Repeat, a little faster.

Book

Now read this bilingual book, which received a 2008 Pura Belpré honor award for illustration:

> Gonzalez, Maya Christina. *My Colors, My World / Mis colores, mi mundo*. Children's Book Press, 2007.

Rhyme

Here is a very simple traditional rhyme:

A la escuela y al jardín,	At school and in the garden
Con Martín	With Martin
Colorín.	In the garden.

Additional Books

Add these titles to your display of books for parents to check out:

> Beaton, Clare. *Colors / Los colores*. Barron's, 1997.
>
> Carle, Eric. *Colors / Colores*. Penguin Young Readers Group, 2008.
>
> Cruz, Jimena. *Los colores*. Editorial Sigmar, 2007.
>
> Gaetán, Maura. *Colors / Colores*. Editorial Sigmar, 2006.
>
> Gaetán, Maura. *Un día en colores: Un libro sobre colores*. Editorial Sigmar, 2006.
>
> Gunzi, Christiane. *My Very First Look at Colors*. Two-Can Publishing, 1997. Spanish: *Mi primera mirada a los colores*. Two-Can Publishing, 2004.
>
> Martín Gimeno, Lourdes. *Conoce los colores*. Susaeta, 2005.
>
> Rigol, Francesc. *Colores*. Susaeta, 2005.

Closing Rhyme

End your program with a closing rhyme or song. Be sure to send home a flier with the titles of the books you read, the words to the songs and rhymes, and a list of reading tips.

PROGRAM 4: THE FARM / *LA GRANJA*

Opening Rhyme

Begin your program with your welcome rhyme in Spanish and English. Invite parents to participate with their children.

Vocabulary Activity

Talk about the farm and ask the toddlers what kind of animals they might see at the farm. You can have pictures of animals that the toddlers can identify. Here are a few of the animals you might find on the farm.

la gallina	the hen
el gallo	the rooster
el cerdo	the pig
el caballo	the horse
la vaca	the cow

Book

Share this first book, always introducing the title, the author, and the illustrator:

Luján, Jorge Elias. *Rooster / Gallo*. Groundwood Books, 2004.

Song

You can sing "Old MacDonald Had a Farm" in English and then follow up with the song "La granja" in Spanish by the Mexican children's musician José-Luis Orozco:

LA GRANJA	THE FARM
Vengan a ver mi granja que es hermosa.	Come and see my farm, for it is beautiful.
Vengan a ver mi granja que es hermosa.	Come and see my farm, for it is beautiful.
El patito hace así, cuá, cuá	The duckling goes like this, quack, quack.
El patito hace así, cuá, cuá	The duckling goes like this, quack, quack.

CORO	CHORUS
Oh, vengan, amigos,	Oh, come, my friends,
Vengan, amigos,	Oh, come, my friends,
Vengan, amigos, vengan.	Oh, come to see my farm.
(Cantar dos veces.)	*(Sing twice.)*

Repeat the song, inserting the following animals:

El pollito hace así, pío, pío.	The chick goes like this, peep, peep.
La vaquita hace así, mú, mú.	The calf goes like this, moo, moo.

El puerquito hace así, oinc, oinc.	The piglet goes like this, oink, oink.
El burrito hace así, íja, íja.	The donkey goes like this, hee-haw, hee-haw.
El gallito hace así, kikiri, kí.	The rooster goes like this, cock-a-doodle-doo.

Book

Here is another book to use with your group of toddlers:

Pietrapiana, Christian. *Tomasa the Cow / La vaca Tomasa*. Arte Público Press, 1999.

Song

Here is a traditional song to sing. You can ask parents to sit their toddler on their lap and recite it as a bouncing rhyme.

CABALLITO BLANCO	WHITE PONY
Caballito blanco,	White pony,
Sácame de aquí,	Give me a ride,
Llévame a mi pueblo	Take me to the town
Donde yo nací.	Where I was born.
Tengo, tengo, tengo,	I have, I have, I have,
Tú no tienes nada.	you have nothing.
Tengo tres ovejas	I have three sheep
En una manada.	In my herd.
Una me da leche,	One gives me milk,
Otra me da lana,	One gives me wool,
Otra mantequilla	One gives me butter
Para la semana.	That lasts me all week.

Book

Next, you can read Pat Hutchins's classic tale about Rosie the hen:

Hutchins, Pat. *Rosie's Walk*. Simon and Schuster Children's Publishing, 1968. Spanish: *El paseo de Rosie*. Simon and Schuster Children's Publishing, 1997.

Song

Here is an action song. Before each stanza, practice walking first like a duck, then like a chicken, and then like a lamb.

LOS ANIMALITOS	THE LITTLE ANIMALS
Detrás de Doña Pata	After Mrs. Duck
Corren los patitos;	Run the little ducklings;
Por allí, por allá,	This way and that way,
Cuá, cuá, cuá.	Quack, quack, quack.
Detrás de Doña Gallina	After Mrs. Chicken
Siguen los pollitos;	The little chicks follow;
Por allí, por allá,	This way and that way,
Pío, pío, pío.	Cheep, cheep, cheep.
Detrás de Doña Borrega	After Mrs. Sheep
Van los borreguitos;	Go the little lambs;
Por allí, por allá,	This way and that way,
Beh, beh, beh.	Baa, baa, baa.

Additional Books

Here are books for your display table. Be sure you tell parents that the books are ready to be checked out to share with their toddlers.

Boynton, Sandra. *Moo, Baa, La La La*. Simon and Schuster, 1984. Spanish: *Muu, beee: ¡Así fue!* Simon and Schuster Libros para Niños, 2003.

Brown, Margaret Wise. *Big Red Barn*. HarperCollins, 1994. Spanish: *El gran granero rojo*. HarperCollins, 1996.

Busquets, Jordi. *Mis amigos de la granja*. Susaeta, 2005.

Dupuis, Sylvia. *Las diez gallinas*. Edelvives/Editorial Luis Vives, 2006.

Espinoza, Gerald. *Los pollitos dicen*. Ediciones Ekaré, 2007.

Inaraja, Javier. *La granja*. Susaeta, 2005.

Rigol, Francesc. *Animales de la granja*. Susaeta, 2005.

Closing Rhyme

End your program with a closing rhyme or song. Be sure to send home a flier with the titles of the books you read, the words to the songs and rhymes, and a list of reading tips.

PROGRAM 5: BUGS / *LOS INSECTOS*

Opening Rhyme

Begin your program with your welcome rhyme in Spanish and English. Invite parents to participate with their children.

Book

If you have older toddlers, you might want to try reading each page of this book. If you have younger toddlers, read select lines of text. It is a good story to learn and then tell, and it has big, beautiful illustrations. You can have your kids repeat Martina's full name with you: Martina Josefina Catalina Cucaracha.

> Deedy, Carmen Agra. *Martina, the Beautiful Cockroach: A Cuban Folktale.* Peachtree, 2007. Spanish: *Martina, una cucarachita muy linda.* Peachtree, 2007.

Song

Next, sing this popular song about a thirsty cockroach:

LA CUCARACHA	THE COCKROACH
La cucaracha, la cucaracha,	The cockroach, the cockroach
Ya no puede caminar.	Can no longer walk around.
Porque le falta, porque le falta,	Because he needs some, because he needs some,
Limonada que tomar	Lemonade to drink

Book

Butterflies are beautiful, and you might want to show pictures of butterflies before you read one of the following stories. The first title, about a young boy named Olmo, is available only in Spanish. Read it in Spanish and then have the toddlers and their parents tell you the story in English.

> Ada, Alma Flor. *Olmo y la mariposa azul.* Laredo Publishing, 1992.
> Brown, Monica. *Butterflies on Carmen Street / Mariposas en la calle Carmen.* Arte Público Press, 2007.

Movement Rhyme

Here's a rhyme about a spider that went for a walk. Make a spiderweb on the floor using masking tape. Play follow the leader with the toddlers, and you can be Doña or Don Araña as you walk around the spiderweb. Be sure to dance during the third line and then you can start walking backward until you ask your toddlers to take a seat.

DOÑA ARAÑA	DOÑA ARAÑA
Doña Araña se fue a pasear	Doña Araña went for a walk
Hizo un hilo y se puso a trepar.	and swung happily from her web.
Vino el viento y la hizo bailar.	Along came the wind, which made her dance.
Vino la tormenta y la hizo bajar.	Along came a storm, so she had to go back.

Book

If you can, bring in an ant farm and let your toddlers see ants at work, then read this story:

> Ramirez, Michael Rose. *The Little Ant / La hormiga chiquita*. Rizzoli, 1995.

Motion Rhyme

Here is a motion rhyme. Sing this several times using hand motions.

LA HUITSI HUITSI ARAÑA	THE ITSY BITSY SPIDER
La huitsi huitsi araña	The itsy bitsy spider
Subió, subió, subió.	Went up the waterspout.
Vino la lluvia y	Down came the rain
Se la llevó.	And washed the spider out.
Salió el sol y	Out came the sun and
Todo lo secó.	Dried up all the rain.
Y la huitsi huitsi araña	And the itsy bitsy spider
Subió, subió, subió.	Went up the spout again.

You can substitute *hormiguita,* or "little ant," for *araña* and use two fingers to make the motion of the ant walking up the waterspout.

LA HORMIGUITA	THE ITSY BITSY ANT
La hormiguita	The itsy bitsy ant
Subió, subió, subió.	Went up the waterspout.
Vino la lluvia y	Down came the rain
Se la llevó.	And washed the little ant out.
Salió el sol y	Out came the sun and
Todo lo secó.	Dried up all the rain.

| Y la hormiguita | And the itsy bitsy ant |
| Subió, subió, subió. | Went up the spout again. |

Additional Books

Here are a few books to add to your stack. You can make substitutions for any of these or have them available for your storytime customers:

Carle, Eric. *The Very Busy Spider.* Philomel Books, 1984. Spanish: *La araña muy ocupada.* Philomel Books, 2008.

Carle, Eric. *The Very Hungry Caterpillar.* Philomel Books, 1987. Spanish: *La oruga muy hambrienta.* Philomel Books, 1989.

Facklam, Margery. *Bugs for Lunch / Insectos para el almuerzo.* Charlesbridge, 2002.

McDonald, Jill. *The Itsy Bitsy Spider.* Scholastic, 2007. Spanish: *La araña chiquitita.* Scholastic, 2007.

Prims, Marta. *I Am a Little Spider / Soy una pequeña araña.* Barron's, 2002.

Robleda, Margarita. *Un grillo en mi cocina.* Sitesa, 1992.

Closing Rhyme

End your program with a closing rhyme or song. Be sure to send home a flier with the titles of the books you read, the words to the songs and rhymes, and a list of reading tips.

PROGRAM 6: OPPOSITES / *LOS OPUESTOS*

Opening Rhyme

Begin your program with your welcome rhyme in Spanish and English. Invite parents to participate with their children.

Vocabulary Activity

Talk about opposites and give some examples.

arriba / up	*abajo* / down
despierto / awake	*dormido* / asleep
feliz / happy	*triste* / sad

Book

Read this bilingual story with the toddlers:

>   Cumpiano, Ina. *Quinito, Day and Night / Quinito, día y noche.*
>   Children's Book Press, 2008.

Rhyme

Here is a simple rhyme to share with the group:

SALTAR	JUMP
Salto por aquí,	I'll jump over here,
Salto por allá,	I'll jump over there,
Pues esa culebra	'Cause that snake's a fright
No me ha de picar.	And I won't let him bite.

Book

Next, share this book:

>   Cruz, Jimena. *Los opuestos.* Editorial Sigmar, 2007.

Vocabulary Activity

Talk to the toddlers again about opposites. Here are more examples to show.

grande/big	*chico*/small
blanco/white	*negro*/black
flaco/skinny	*gordo*/fat
mojado/wet	*seco*/dry
alto/tall	*pequeño*/small
arriba/above	*abajo*/below
sí/yes	*no*/no

Book

One more book about opposites to try is this one:

>   Gaetán, Maura. *Opuestos.* Editorial Sigmar, 2006.

Call-and-Response Rhyme

Try this rhyme as a call-and-response:

LOS OPUESTOS	OPPOSITES
Yo digo nuevo, tú dices viejo.	I say new, you say old.
Yo digo arriba, tú dices abajo.	I say up, you say down.
Yo digo frío, tú dices calor.	I say cold, you say hot.
Yo digo dormido, tú dices despierto.	I say sleep, you say awake.

Additional Books

Here are a few more books about opposites that you can display for parents to check out:

Emberly, Rebecca. *My Opposites / Mis opuestos*. Little, Brown, 2000.

Figuerola, Mercedes. *Los contrarios*. Susaeta, 2005.

Ranchetti, Sebastiano. *Animal Opposites / Opuestos animales*. Gareth Stevens Publishing, 2008.

Suárez, Maribel. *Los contrarios*. Editorial Grijalbo, 1990.

Closing Rhyme

End your program with a closing rhyme or song. Be sure to send home a flier with the titles of the books you read, the words to the songs and rhymes, and a list of reading tips.

PROGRAM 7: THE SENSES / *LOS SENTIDOS*

Opening Rhyme

Begin your program with your welcome rhyme in Spanish and English. Invite parents to participate with their children.

Vocabulary Activity

Talk about the five senses—sight, hearing, touch, smell, and taste. In Spanish they are *la vista, el oído, el tacto, el olfato,* and *el gusto.*

Book

Start with the following book available in Spanish and in English:

Shannon, David. *David Smells!* Scholastic, 2005. Spanish: *¡David huele!* Blue Sky Press, 2005.

Call-and-Response Rhyme

Here's a rhyme to recite that you can do as a call-and-response, first in Spanish and then in English:

MIS CINCO SENTIDOS	MY FIVE SENSES
Una boquita para comer,	A small mouth for eating,
Mi naricita para oler,	My little nose for smelling,
Mis dos ojitos para ver,	My two little eyes for seeing,
Mis dos orejitas para oír,	My two little ears for hearing,
Mis dos manitas para tocar,	My two little hands for touching,
¿Y mi cabecita?	And my head?
Para dormir.	For sleeping.

Book

This next book is about taste. Although it is available only in Spanish, you can read through it once and then have your toddlers and parents help you by telling you what they see on each page in English.

Suárez, Maribel. *¿A qué sabe? El sentido del gusto*. Editorial Grijalbo, 1995.

Rhyme

Now ask your group of toddlers to point to their mouth, nose, eyes, ears, and head when you say each one and then to repeat after you with this simple rhyme.

Una boca para comer,	One mouth to eat,
Una nariz para oler.	One nose to smell,
Dos ojos para ver,	Two eyes to see,
Dos orejas para oír,	Two ears to hear,
Y una cabeza para dormir.	And one head to sleep.

Book

If your group is doing well with attention and participation, share a third book. You will be the best to decide on when to stop.

Cousins, Lucy. *What Can Pinky Hear?* Candlewick Press, 1997.
Spanish: *¿Qué puede oír Blas?* Serres, 1997.

Motion Rhyme

Next, you can share this motion rhyme and do all the motions with your group:

MIS MANITAS	MY LITTLE HANDS
Tengo dos manitas.	I have two little hands.
Dos manitas especiales.	Two very special little hands.
Pueden aplaudir.	They can clap.
Pueden girar.	They can roll.
Y pueden abrazarse	And they can give each other a hug
Como dos amigas.	Just like two friends.

Additional Books

The following books can be shared with parents as you encourage them to check them out:

Fernández, Laura. *¿Qué veo? El sentido de la vista.* Grijalbo, 1995.

Sobrino, Javier. *Me gusta.* Kókinos, 2002.

Closing Rhyme

End your program with a closing rhyme or song. Be sure to send home a flier with the titles of the books you read, the words to the songs and rhymes, and a list of reading tips.

PROGRAM 8: TRANSPORTATION / *EL TRANSPORTE*

Opening Rhyme

Begin your program with your welcome rhyme in Spanish and English. Invite parents to participate with their children.

Vocabulary Activity

You can talk about different types of transportation. You can borrow a few toys like a car, a boat, a bicycle, and an airplane, or you can show pictures of these items. Identify each item in Spanish and in English.

el barco	boat
el coche	car
el avión	airplane

la bicicleta	bicycle
el metro	subway
el taxi	taxi

Book

Read this book about Maisy that is available in Spanish and in English:

> Cousins, Lucy. *How Will You Get There, Maisy?* Candlewick Press, 2004. Spanish: *¿Cómo irá, Maisy?* Serres, 2004.

Song

This next song was first translated into Spanish by the musician José-Luis Orozco. I have combined his version with one I learned. Sing this song and do all the motions with your toddlers:

LAS RUEDAS DEL CAMIÓN	THE WHEELS ON THE BUS
Las ruedas del camión van	The wheels on the bus go
Dando vueltas,	Round and round,
Dando vueltas,	Round and round,
Dando vueltas,	Round and round.
Las ruedas del camión van	The wheels on the bus go
Dando vueltas,	Round and round,
Por la ciudad.	All through the town.
La gente en el camión	The people on the bus go
Salta y salta . . .	Up and down . . .
Los limpiadores del camión hacen	The wipers on the bus go
Swish, swish, swish . . .	Swish, swish, swish . . .
Las monedas del camion hacen	The money on the bus goes
Clinc, clinc, clinc . . .	Plink, plink, plink . . .
El bebé en el camión hace,	The baby on the bus goes,
"Ña, ña, ña . . ."	"Waa, waa, waa . . ."
La mamá en el camión hace,	The mother on the bus goes,
"Shish, shish, shish . . ."	"Shh, shh, shh . . ."

El chofer en el camión dice,	The driver on the bus says,
"Pasen para atrás . . ."	"Move on back . . ."
Las puertas del camión	The doors on the bus go
Se abren y se cierran . . .	Open and shut . . .
Las ruedas del camión van . . .	The wheels on the bus go . . .

Book

Next, you can share this bilingual book:

> Luciani, Brigitte. *How Will We Get to the Beach? / ¿Cómo iremos a la playa?* North-South Books, 2003.

Song

Sing this song or recite it as a call-and-response rhyme:

VAMOS A REMAR	ROW YOUR BOAT
Ven, ven, ven acá	Row, row, row your boat
Vamos a remar	Gently down the stream
Rema, que rema, que rema, que rema,	Merrily, merrily, merrily, merrily
La vida es como un sueño.	Life is but a dream.

Book

Another book that you might share is this one about Teresa and her shiny new car, a gift from her grandpa:

> Soto, Gary. *My Little Car / Mi carrito.* Putnam's, 2006.

Rhyme

This is a traditional nonsense rhyme that rhymes in Spanish but certainly loses the rhyme in the English translation:

EL QUE SE FUE A SEVILLA	HE WHO WENT TO SEVILLE
El que se fue a Sevilla	He who went to Seville
Perdió su silla.	Lost his chair.
El que se fue a Aragón	He who went to Aragon
Perdió su sillón.	Lost the whole sofa.

Additional Books

Here are some books to have on hand for parents to check out:

Blackstone, Stella. *Bear on a Bike.* Barefoot Books, 2001. Spanish: *Oso en bicicleta.* Barefoot Books, 2003.

Busquets, Jordi. *Hoy vamos de viaje.* Susaeta, 2005.

Denou, Violeta. *Teo descubre los medios de transporte.* Grupo Editorial Ceac, 1998.

Denou, Violeta. *Teo en avión.* Planeta Publishing, 2004.

Denou, Violeta. *Teo encuentra los errores: Un paseo en barco.* Grupo Editorial Ceac, 2000.

Denou, Violeta. *Teo se va de viaje.* Planeta Publishing, 2004.

Franco, Betsy. *Vamos a la granja de la abuela.* Children's Press, 2003.

Closing Rhyme

End your program with a closing rhyme or song. Be sure to send home a flier with the titles of the books you read, the words to the songs and rhymes, and a list of reading tips.

Chapter 4

PROGRAMS FOR PRESCHOOLERS
PROGRAMS PARA NIÑOS PREESCOLARES

Shy, rambunctious, inquisitive, and *playful* are words that can describe many preschoolers. You are certain to have kids who fall into each of these categories. They love attention and give attention. They are able to sit still for a longer period of time. Twenty to thirty minutes is a good amount of time to plan for your program. Again, plenty of variety will hold their interest. Repetition is good, and it is OK to read the same books two or three times during the same program with the same group. You may want to read a book to the group first. Next, take one page at a time and ask questions. For the third reading, have the children tell you the story sequence. These are all good basic skills. Fingerplays are easier, and you might want to encourage parents to help their children with the finger motions.

Plan an opening activity that the children will grasp easily, and they will always be ready when they enter your storytime area. Here is one that will be familiar:

SI ESTÁS FELIZ	IF YOU'RE HAPPY
Si estás feliz y lo sabes,	If you're happy and you know it,
Aplaudirás.	Clap your hands.
Si estás feliz y lo sabes,	If you're happy and you know it,
Aplaudirás.	Clap your hands.
Si estás feliz y lo sabes,	If you're happy and you know it,
Tu cara lo mostrará.	Then your face will really show it.
Si estás feliz y lo sabes,	If you're happy and you know it,
Aplaudirás.	Clap your hands.

PROGRAM 1: ANIMALS / *LOS ANIMALES*

Opening Rhyme

Start your program with your opening rhyme. Feel free to find a different one from "Si estás feliz / If You're Happy."

Vocabulary Activity

You can start this program with animal sounds. Let the preschoolers know that animals sound different depending on where they live. A duck living in Mexico doesn't say, "Quack, quack." Instead, the duck says, "Cuá, cuá."

El burro dice jijaaa, jijaaa.	The donkey says hee-haw, hee-haw.
La gallina dice cara cara, cara cara.	The hen says cluck, cluck.
El pollito dice pío, pío.	The chick says peep, peep.
La vaca dice muu.	The cow says moo.
El perrito dice guau guau.	The puppy says bowwow.
El patito dice cuá cuá.	The duckling says quack, quack.
La oveja dice behhh, behhh.	The sheep says baa, baa.
El pavo dice gluglú, gluglú.	The turkey says gobble, gobble.
El gallo dice kikirikí.	The rooster says cock-a-doodle-doo.

Book

Borreguita is a little lamb that is able to outwit Señor Coyote in this first story to share. A Spanish and English edition is available.

Aardema, Verna. *Borreguita and the Coyote.* Knopf, 1996. Spanish: *Borreguita y el coyote.* Harcourt, 1997.

Rhyme

You can recite this silly traditional rhyme with the group, and then you can distribute musical instruments and kids can pretend to be the *lobitos*.

CINCO LOBITOS	FIVE LITTLE WOLVES
Cinco lobitos	Mama wolf
Tiene la loba.	Has five baby wolves.
Blancos y negros	White ones and black ones
Detrás de la toba.	Behind the big rock.
Uno le canta	One sings

Todo el día,	All day long,
Y los otros le tocan	And the others play
La sinfonía.	The symphony.

Book

Next, read this southwestern version of "The Three Little Pigs." Be sure to take time to point out the drawings and some of the titles on the pig's bookshelf. Your group is sure to enjoy José, the big bad wolf, and will be happy to repeat after you, "No way, José" when José asks each pig to let him in.

> Salinas, Bobbi. *The Three Pigs / Los tres cerdos: Nacho, Tito, and Miguel.* Piñata Publications, 1998.

Song

You can engage your group in this song about ten little pigs, which is adapted from the traditional song about ten little puppies. You will find that song later on in this book. You might want to engage your group of preschoolers to tell you what animal to sing about. Instead of pigs, you might sing about kittens, cows, or horses.

LOS DIEZ CERDITOS	TEN LITTLE PIGS
Yo tenía diez cerditos,	I had ten little pigs.
Uno se perdió a la nieve;	One got lost in the snow;
Ya no más me quedan nueve.	Now I only have nine.
De los nueve que quedaban,	Of the nine I had left,
Uno se comió un bizcocho;	One ate a biscuit;
Ya no más me quedan ocho.	Now I only have eight.
De los ocho que quedaban,	Of the eight I had left,
Uno fue por un juguete;	One left to find a toy;
Ya no más me quedan siete.	Now I only have seven.
De los siete que quedaban,	Of the seven I had left,
Uno se quemó los pies;	One burned his feet;
Ya no más me quedan seis.	Now I only have six.
De los seis que quedaban,	Of the six I had left,
Uno se fue brinco y brinco;	One jumped away;
Ya no más me quedan cinco.	Now I only have five.

De los cinco que quedaban,	Of the five I had left,
Uno se marchó al teatro;	One marched off to the theater;
Ya no más me quedan cuatro.	Now I only have four.
De los cuatro que quedaban,	Of the four I had left,
Uno se volteó al revés;	One turned backward;
Ya no más me quedan tres.	Now I only have three.
De los tres que quedaban,	Of the three I had left,
Uno fue a comprar arroz;	One left to buy rice;
Ya no más me quedan dos.	Now I only have two.
De los dos que quedaban,	Of the two I had left,
Uno se murió de ayuno;	One died of starvation;
Ya no más me queda uno.	Now I only have one.
Este uno que quedaba,	Of the one I had left,
Se lo llevó mi cuñada;	My sister-in-law took one;
Ya no me queda nada.	Now I don't have any.
Cuando ya no tenía nada,	And when I didn't have any,
La mamá crió otra vez;	Mama Pig conceived again;
Y ahora tengo otros diez.	And now I have ten others.

Book

This book is available in Spanish and in English:

> Paparone, Pamela. *Five Little Ducks*. North-South Books, 2005.
> Spanish: *Los cinco patitos*. North-South Books, 2007.

Song

Imagine what you can buy for half a peso! This traditional song will give you some ideas; you might find it on a CD by another title, "Con real y medio." It is the same tune.

CON MEDIO PESO	WITH HALF A PESO
Con medio peso compré	With half a peso, I bought
una burra	a donkey
Y la burra tuvo burrito.	And that donkey had a baby.
Tengo burra, tengo burrito,	I have a donkey, I have her baby,
Y siempre todo con medio peso.	And all of this for half a peso.

Con medio peso compré
    una pava

With half a peso, I bought
    a turkey

Y la pava tuvo pavito.

And that turkey had a baby.

Tengo pava, tengo pavito,

I have a turkey, I have her baby,

Y siempre todo con medio peso.

And all of this for half a peso.

Con medio peso compré
    una pata

With half a peso, I bought
    a duck

Y la pata tuvo patito.

And that duck had a duckling.

Tengo pata, tengo patito,

I have a duck, I have her duckling,

Y siempre todo con medio peso.

And all of this for half a peso.

Con medio peso compré
    una gata

With half a peso, I bought a cat

Y la gata tuvo gatita.

And that cat had a kitten.

Tengo gata, tengo gatita,

I have a cat, I have her kitten,

Y siempre todo con medio peso.

And all of this for half a peso.

Con medio peso compré
    una loba

With half a peso, I bought a wolf

Y la loba tuvo lobita.

And that wolf had a pup.

Tengo loba, tengo lobita,

I have a wolf, I have her pup,

Y siempre todo con medio peso.

And all of this for half a peso.

Con medio peso compré
    una polla

With half a peso, I bought a hen

Y la polla tuvo pollita.

And that hen had a chick.

Tengo polla, tengo pollita,

I have a hen, I have her chick,

Y siempre todo con medio peso.

And all of this for half a peso.

You can keep adding animals, such as in the following:

caballo, caballito	horse, pony
baca, vaquita	cow, calf
oso, osito	bear, cub
cerdo, cerdito	pig, piglet

Book

If you find that your preschoolers are ready for another story, you might want to try this one:

Tafolla, Carmen. *Baby Coyote and the Old Lady / El coyotito y la viejita: A Bilingual Story.* Wings Press, 2000.

Song

This next song gives you an opportunity for some action. Use masking tape to make one or several large spiderwebs. Ask the preschoolers to pretend they are elephants with one arm in front of their nose and the other behind them.

UN ELEFANTE	ONE ELEPHANT
Un elefante se columpiaba	One elephant was swinging
Sobre la tela de una araña.	On a spider's web.
Como veía que resistía	He was having so much fun
Fue a llamar a otro elefante.	That he called another to join him.
Dos elefantes se columpiaban	Two elephants were swinging
Sobre la tela de una araña.	On a spider's web.
Como veían que resistía	They were having so much fun
Fueron a llamar a otro elefante.	That they called another to join them.
Tres elefantes . . .	Three elephants . . .

There is another version with the elephants balancing instead of swinging on the spider's web; instead of *columpiaba,* you would say *balanceaba.*

Un elefante se balanceaba	One elephant was balancing
Sobre la tela de una araña.	On a spider's web.
Como veía que resistía	He was having so much fun
Fue a llamar a otro elefante.	That he called another to join him.
Dos elefantes se balanceaban	Two elephants were balancing
Sobre la tela de una araña.	On a spider's web.
Como veían que resistía	They were having so much fun
Fueron a llamar a	That they called another
otro elefante.	to join them.
Tres elefantes . . .	Three elephants . . .

Additional Books

Here are a few other books that you can suggest for parents to check out and read at home with their preschoolers:

Ada, Alma Flor. *La hamaca de la vaca, o, Un amigo mas.* Santillana USA, 2000.

Banks, Kate. *Fox.* Farrar, Straus, and Giroux, 2007. Spanish: *El zorrito.* Editorial Juventud, 2007.

Delacre, Lulu. *Nathan's Balloon Adventure.* Scholastic, 1991.

Closing Rhyme

You started your program with a rhyme, and you can end with the same rhyme or try something different.

PROGRAM 2: THE NEIGHBORHOOD / *EL BARRIO*

Opening Rhyme

Start your program with your opening rhyme.

Book

This next story is about a stranger who brings along his rooster when he moves into a new neighborhood:

Villaseñor, Victor. *The Stranger and the Red Rooster / El forastero y el gallo rojo.* Piñata Books, 2006.

Game

The following is a circle game or *ronda,* as it is called in Spanish. Children in Mexico play this game in the street in front of their houses. Have your group form a circle and hold hands. Then everyone walks around in a circle in one direction. On the last line, call out a child's name. That child leads the circle going the opposite way. Continue until each child has had a turn.

LA RUEDA DE SAN MIGUEL	THE CIRCLE OF SAN MIGUEL
A la rueda, la rueda de	In the circle, the circle of
San Miguel, San Miguel,	San Miguel, San Miguel,
Todos traen su caja de miel.	Everyone's bringing their box of honey.
A lo maduro, a lo maduro,	Ripen, ripen,
Que se volteé,	Turn around,
Que se volteé,	Turn around,
¡(Nombre del niño) de burro!	(Child's name) is the donkey!

Book

Lupita wants a kite and her grandpa helps her make one. You might want to tell your group that another more common word for "kite" in Spanish is *cometa:*

> Ruiz-Flores, Lupe. *Lupita's Papalote / El papalote de Lupita.* Piñata
> Books, 2002.

Game

Gather your preschoolers and play follow the leader. You will be Comadre Juana or Compadre Juan. Dance your way around the room. In Latin American countries, this is a traditional circle game:

LA COMADRE JUANA	COMADRE JUANA
La comadre Juana estaba	Comadre Juana
En un baile, que lo baile, que lo baile,	Was in a dance, dance, dance,
Y si no lo baila le doy	And if she doesn't dance,
Castigo de agua.	I will get her wet.
Qué baile usted que la quiero ver bailar.	Dance, I want to see you dance.
Alzando los pies en el aire	Lifting her feet in the air
Pero bien que la baila usted.	You dance it so well.
Déjenla sola, sola en el baile.	Leave her alone, alone in the dance.
La, la, la, la, la . . .	La, la, la, la, la . . .

Book

Here is another book to share:

> Urdaneta, Josefina. *Busca que te busca.* Playco Editores, 2000.

Song

This next song gives you an opportunity to pass out musical instruments that your preschoolers can use after you sing together. José-Luis Orozco has a version of this song called "La pulga de San Jose" on one of his CDs.

LA FERIA DE SAN JUAN	THE FAIR OF SAN JUAN
En la feria de San Juan	At the fair of San Juan
Yo compré una guitarra,	I bought a guitar,
Tarra, tarra, tarra, la guitarra.	Tar, tar, tar, the guitar.

Venga usted, venga usted,	Go yourself, go yourself,
A la feria de San Juan,	To the fair of San Juan,
Venga usted, venga usted,	Go yourself, go yourself,
A la feria de San Juan.	To the fair of San Juan.
En la feria de San Juan	At the fair of San Juan,
Yo compré un violín,	I bought a violin,
lin, lin, lin, el violín,	Lin, lin, lin, the violin,
Tarra, tarra, tarra, la guitarra.	Tar, tar, tar, the guitar.
Venga usted, venga usted,	Go yourself, go yourself,
A la feria de San Juan,	To the fair of San Juan,
Venga usted, venga usted,	Go yourself, go yourself,
A la feria de San Juan.	To the fair of San Juan.
En la feria de San Juan	At the fair of San Juan,
Yo compré un violón,	I bought a viola,
Lon, lon, lon, el violón,	La, la, la, the viola,
Lin, lin, lin, el violín,	Lin, lin, lin, the violin,
Tarra, tarra, tarra, la guitarra.	Tar, tar, tar, the guitar.
Venga usted, venga usted,	Go yourself, go yourself,
A la feria de San Juan,	To the fair of San Juan,
Venga usted, venga usted,	Go yourself, go yourself,
A la feria de San Juan.	To the fair of San Juan.
En la feria de San Juan	At the fair of San Juan,
Yo compré un tambor,	I bought a drum,
Pom, pom, el tambor,	Boom, boom, the drum,
Lon, lon, lon, el violón,	La, la, la, the viola,
Lin, lin, lin, el violín,	Lin, lin, lin, the violin,
Tarra, tarra, tarra, la guitarra.	Tar, tar, tar, the guitar.
Venga usted, venga usted,	Go yourself, go yourself,
A la feria de San Juan,	To the fair of San Juan,
Venga usted, venga usted,	Go yourself, go yourself,
A la feria de San Juan.	To the fair of San Juan.

Book

You can read one more story if your group is still attentive. This one shows
how people of different cultures share many similarities:

Tabor, Nancy Maria Grande. *We Are a Rainbow / Somos un arco iris.* Charlesbridge, 1997.

Song

Next, sing this traditional Latin song. The title means "beautiful little sky."

CIELITO LINDO	CIELITO LINDO
Ay, ay, ay, ay,	Ay, ay, ay, ay,
Canta y no llores.	Sing and don't cry.
Porque cantando se alegran,	If you sing, your heart
Cielito lindo, los corazones.	Will be happy, Cielito Lindo.
Ese lunar que tienes, cielito lindo,	The beauty mark that you have
Junto a la boca,	Close to your mouth,
No se lo des a nadie,	Don't give it to anybody,
Cielito lindo,	Cielito Lindo,
Que a mí me toca.	Because I want it.
Ay, ay, ay, ay,	Ay, ay, ay, ay,
Canta y no llores.	Sing and don't cry.
Porque cantando se alegran,	If you sing, your heart
Cielito lindo, los corazones.	Will be happy, Cielito Lindo.
De la Sierra Morena, cielito lindo,	Down from the Sierra Morena,
Vienen bajando	Cielito Lindo,
Un par de ojitos negros,	Come a pair of beautiful
Cielito lindo, de contrabando.	Dark eyes of contraband.
Ay, ay, ay, ay,	Ay, ay, ay, ay,
Canta y no llores.	Sing and don't cry.
Porque cantando se alegran,	If you sing, your heart
Cielito lindo, los corazones.	Will be happy, Cielito Lindo.

Additional Books

Here are a few books for your display area that you can encourage parents to check out:

Ancona, George. *Barrio: José's Neighborhood.* Harcourt Brace, 1998.
Spanish: *Barrio: El barrio de José.* Harcourt Brace, 1998.

Ancona, George. *My House / Mi casa*. Children's Press, 2004.

Ancona, George. *My Neighborhood / Mi barrio*. Children's Press, 2004.

Argueta, Jorge. *Alfredito Flies Home*. Groundwood Books, 2008.
Spanish: *Alfredito regresa volando a su casa*. Groundwood Books, 2007.

Closing Rhyme

You started your program with a rhyme, and you can end with the same rhyme or try something different.

PROGRAM 3: FOOD / *LA COMIDA*

Opening Rhyme

Start your program with your opening rhyme.

Book

Next, read this story in Spanish and then in English:

Mora, Pat. *Delicious Hullabaloo / Pachanga deliciosa*. Piñata Books, 1998.

Song

Here is the song "Apples and Bananas" in Spanish, which you can sing with your group. In the Spanish version of "Apples and Bananas," the song begins with bananas. *Plátanos* are bananas and *manzanas* are apples. I learned this song from a children's librarian named Ginger Payne.

PLÁTANOS Y MANZANAS	APPLES AND BANANAS
Me gusta comer, comer, comer	I like to eat, eat, eat
Plátanos y manzanas.	Apples and bananas.
Me gusta comer, comer, comer	I like to eat, eat, eat
Plátanos y manzanas.	Apples and bananas.
Ma gasta camar, camar, camar	*(Substitute the letter A for*
Plátanas a manzanas.	*all vowels.)*
Ma gasta camar, camar, camar	
Plátanas a manzanas.	

Me gueste cemer, cemer, cemer   *(Substitute the letter* E *for*
Plétenes e menzenes.   *all vowels.)*
Me geste cemer, cemer, cemer
Plétenes e menzenes.

Mi guiste cimir, cimir, cimir   *(Substitute the letter* I *for*
Plítinis i minzinis.   *all vowels.)*
Mi giste cimir, cimir, cimir
Plítinis i minzinis.

Mo gosto comor, comor, comor   *(Substitute the letter* O *for*
Plótonos o monzonos.   *all vowels.)*
Mo gosto comor, comor, comor
Plótonos o monzonos.

Mu gustu cumur, cumur, cumur   *(Substitute the letter* U *for*
Plútunus u munzunus.   *all vowels.)*
Mu gustu cumur, cumur, cumur
Plútunus u munzunus.

Me gusta comer, comer, comer   I like to eat, eat, eat
Plátanos y manzanas.   Apples and bananas.
Me gusta comer, comer, comer   I like to eat, eat, eat
Plátanos y manzanas.   Apples and bananas.

Book

Next, share this book, which is available in a bilingual edition:

Argueta, Jorge. *The Fiesta of the Tortillas / La fiesta de las tortillas.*
    Alfaguara, 2006.

Activity

Start this activity by talking about tortillas. You might even show pictures of tortillas. Perhaps you can invite a couple of the parents to bring an electric grill to make tortillas. You would make the *masa*, or "dough," during your storytime and give each child a handful to knead and shape. One at a time, each child can take a turn giving his or her tortilla to a parent and watching the tortilla cook on the grill. Be sure you have parents sign permission slips a week in advance so that the children can participate. Tell parents what the ingredients are in case there are food allergies.

Start clapping, hand over hand, showing the motion of tortillas being prepared for cooking.

TORTILLITAS	LITTLE TORTILLAS
Tortillitas para mamá.	Little tortillas for Mommy.
Tortillitas para papá.	Little tortillas for Daddy.
Las quemaditas para mamá.	Toasty burnt ones for Mommy.
Las bonitas para papá.	Perfect round ones for Daddy.

Do this again, this time giving Mamá the perfect round ones.

Tortillitas para papá.	Little tortillas for Daddy.
Tortillitas para mamá.	Little tortillas for Mommy.
Las quemaditas para papá.	Toasty burnt ones for Daddy.
Las bonitas para mamá.	Perfect round ones for Mommy.

Book

Now it's time for tamales, so share this book by Gary Soto, which is available in Spanish and in English:

Soto, Gary. *Too Many Tamales*. Penguin Young Readers Group, 1996.
Spanish: *Qué montón de tamales*. Tandem Library Books, 1996.

Call-and-Response Rhyme

Chant this traditional rhyme as a call-and-response. Try it once and repeat it a little faster. You can recite this a few times, and each time recite it just a little bit faster.

Batir, batir y batir	Beat, beat, beat,
Y el chocolate a subir.	and watch the chocolate foam.

Book

Have you ever eaten huevos rancheros? Try this tale that is available in Spanish and in English:

Czernecki, Stefan. *Huevos Rancheros*. Crocodile Books, 2001.
Spanish: *Huevos rancheros*. Artes de México el Mundo, 2002.

Song

Here's a traditional song to sing about coconuts, or you can recite it as a tongue twister:

> Compadre, cómpreme un coco.   Compadre, buy me a coconut.
> Compadre, no compro coco.   Compadre, I don't buy coconuts.
> Porque como poco coco,   'Cause I eat few coconuts,
> Poco coco compro.   I buy few coconuts.

Additional Books

This list of books is ready for your display area. Please encourage the parents to check them out:

Alcántara, Ricardo. *¡Caramba con los amigos!* Combel, 2000.

Marcuse, Aída E. *A Piece of Bread / Un trozo de pan.* Panamericana Editorial, 2005.

Mora, Pat. *The Desert Is My Mother / El desierto es mi madre.* Piñata Books, 1994.

Closing Rhyme

You started your program with a rhyme, and you can end with the same rhyme or try something different.

PROGRAM 4: SMALL CREATURES / *CRIATURAS PEQUEÑAS*

Opening Rhyme

Start your program with your opening rhyme.

Book

You will have fun sharing this book about Ramón and a sneaky little mouse:

Robleda, Margarita. *Ramón and His Mouse.* Santillana USA, 2004.
    Spanish: *Ramón y su ratón.* Santillana USA, 2004.

Rhyme

This traditional nursery rhyme is simple and can be repeated several times, getting faster each time you repeat it:

UN RATONCITO	A LITTLE MOUSE
Un ratoncito	A little mouse ran
Iba por un arado	To swim in a pond,
Y este cuentecito	And this little story
Ya se ha acabado.	Is now long gone.

Book

Here is another mouse tale:

> Salas-Porras, Pipina. *The Little Mouse / El ratoncito pequeño: A Nursery Rhyme in Spanish and English.* Cinco Puntos Press, 2001.

Rhyme

Follow the mouse tale with this traditional rhyme. Hold up five fingers and wiggle them fast. Wiggle your ears and then your nose. Count out the five mice on one hand and then run them up your shoulder and under your arm.

CINCO RATONCITOS	FIVE LITTLE MICE
Cinco ratoncitos	Five little mice
De colita gris	With gray little tails
Mueven las orejas,	Wiggle their ears,
Mueven la nariz.	And wiggle their nose.
¡Uno, dos, tres, cuatro, cinco!	One, two, three, four, five!
¡Corren al rincón!	They run and hide!
Porque viene el gato,	Because here comes the cat,
A comer el ratón . . .	To eat the mice . . .

Book

Get your group ready to jump like frogs with Robert Kalan's book, available in Spanish and in English:

> Kalan, Robert. *Jump, Frog, Jump!* Greenwillow Books, 1981. Spanish: *¡Salta, ranita, salta!* Greenwillow Books, 1994.

Rhyme

Chime along with this rhyme that uses the vowels in the alphabet.

La ranita soy yo,	I am a little frog,
Glo, glo, glo.	Glo, glo, glo.

El sapito eres tú,	You are the little toad,
Glu, glu, glu.	Glu, glu, glu.
Cantemos así,	We sing like this,
Gli, gli, gli.	Gli, gli, gli.
Que la lluvia se fue,	That the rain will go away,
Gle, gle, gle.	Gle, gle, gle.
Y la ronda se va,	And the round will end,
Gla, gla, gla.	Gla, gla, gla.

Rhyme

You might want to include this traditional rhyme:

LOS RATONES	THE MICE
Arriba y abajo,	Up and down,
Por los callejones,	Through the alleys,
Pasa una ratita	runs a little mouse
Con veinte ratones.	with twenty more behind her.
Unos sin colita	Some without tails,
Y otros muy colones,	Some with long tails,
Unos sin orejas	Some without ears,
Y otros orejones.	Some with big ears.
Unos sin patitas	Some without feet,
Y otros muy patones,	Some with big feet,
Unos sin ojitos	Some without eyes,
Y otros muy ojones.	Some with big eyes.

Additional Books

Display these titles and invite your storytime parents to check them out:

Rondon, Javier. *Absent-Minded Toad*. Kane/Miller, 1994. Spanish: *El sapo distraído*. Sagebrush Education Resources, 1994.

Soto, Gary. *Chato's Kitchen*. Penguin Young Readers Group, 1995. Spanish: *Chato y su cena*. Sagebrush Education Resources, 1997.

Closing Rhyme

You started your program with a rhyme, and you can end with the same rhyme or try something different.

PROGRAM 5: FABLES AND FOLKLORE / *FÁBULAS Y FOLCLORE*

Opening Rhyme

Start your program with your opening rhyme.

Book

Share this folktale. You may want to first tell your group what a folktale is. Tell the children that many folktales are handed down from one generation to another and that folktales can be similar in different countries.

> Ada, Alma Flor. *The Lizard and the Sun / La lagartija y el sol: A Folktale in English and Spanish*. Bantam Books, 1997.

Song

Sing this traditional Latin American song about a mouse who accidentally irons her tail!

LA PLANCHADORA	THE LAUNDRESS
Una rata vieja	A little old mouse
Que era planchadora,	Spent her days ironing.
Por planchar su falda	She burned her tail
Se quemó la cola.	While ironing her skirt.
Se pusó pomada	She put on a salve
Se amarró un trapito	And tied a bandage on her tail,
Y a la pobre vieja	And the poor little mouse
Le quedó un rabito.	Ended up with a shorter tail.

Book

Move over, three little pigs, because here come the three javelinas in this southwestern tale. Javelinas are peccaries or wild boars and are found in the southwestern United States. They resemble pigs and are aggressive mammals.

> Lowell, Susan. *The Three Javelinas / Los tres pequeños jabalíes*. Northland, 1996.

Tongue Twister

Tongue twisters can be fun. In Spanish they are called *trabalenguas*. Here's one to try with your group. Make sure to start out slow and repeat several times. Each time go a little faster.

Pepe Pecas pica papas	Peter Piper picked a peck of pickled peppers.
Con un pico.	If Peter Piper picked a peck of pickled peppers,
Con un pico	How many pickled peppers
Pica papas Pepe Pecas.	did Peter Piper pick?

Book

Juan Bobo gets mixed up easily. He does things literally, almost like the character Amelia Bedelia. Read this book, which is available in Spanish and in English:

> Montes, Marisa. *Juan Bobo Goes to Work*. HarperCollins, 2000.
> Spanish: *Juan Bobo busca trabajo*. HarperCollins, 2006.

Rhyme

The mouse in this rhyme is like Juan Bobo. There he goes carrying off the entire drawer!

Corre la rata.	There goes the mouse.
Corre el ratón.	Here goes the mouse.
Corre la rata	Carrying off everything,
Con todo y cajón.	Including a drawer.

Additional Books

Here are a few books to add to your display area. Be sure to search for others.

> Nazoa, Aquiles. *Fábula de la ratoncita presumida*. Ediciones Ekaré–Banco del Libro, 1990.
>
> Soto, Gary. *The Old Man and His Door*. Sagebrush Education Resources, 1998. Spanish: *El viejo y su puerta*. Sagebrush Education Resources, 2003.
>
> Tello, Jerry. *Abuelo and the Three Bears / Abuelo y los tres osos*. Scholastic, 1997.

Closing Rhyme

You started your program with a rhyme, and you can end with the same rhyme or try something different.

PROGRAM 6: FAMILY / *LA FAMILIA*

Opening Rhyme

Start your program with your opening rhyme.

Book

Tía has a birthday, and a special surprise awaits her in this first story:

> Mora, Pat. *A Birthday Basket for Tía*. Maxwell Macmillan
> International, 1992. Spanish: *Canasta de cumpleaños para Tía*.
> Lectorum Publications, 1992.

Song

Children form a circle and participate in all the movements to this traditional song that is sung and played as a circle game. Have them say, "Ooh la la!" I have combined the version I learned with one sung by the musician José-Luis Orozco.

LA TÍA MÓNICA	AUNT MONICA
Yo tengo una tía,	I have a lovely aunt,
La Tía Mónica.	Aunt Monica.
Y cuando va de compras	And when she goes shopping
Le dicen, "¡Ooh la la!"	People say, "Ooh la la!"
¡Ooh la la!	Ooh la la!
Así mueve la cadera,	Here's how she moves her hips,
Así, así, así.	Like this, like this, like this.
Así mueve la cadera,	Here's how she moves her hips,
La Tía Mónica.	Our lovely Aunt Monica.
Yo tengo una tía,	I have a lovely aunt,
La Tía Mónica.	Aunt Monica.
Y cuando va de compras	And when she goes shopping
Le dicen, "¡Ooh la la!"	People say, "Ooh la la!"
¡Ooh la la!	Ooh la la!
Así mueve los hombros,	Here's how she moves her shoulders,
Así, así, así.	Like this, like this, like this.
Así mueve los hombros,	Here's how she moves her shoulders,
La Tía Mónica.	Our lovely Aunt Monica.

Yo tengo una tía,	Oh, I have a lovely aunt,
La Tía Mónica.	Monica is her name.
Que cuando va de compras	And when she goes shopping
Le dicen, "¡Ooh la la!"	People say, "Ooh la la!"
¡Ooh la la!	Ooh la la!
Así mueve la cabeza . . .	Here's how she moves her head . . .
Así mueve los pies . . .	Here's how she moves her feet . . .
Así mueve las manos . . .	Here's how she moves her hands . . .
Así se mueve todo el cuerpo . . .	Here's how she moves all over . . .

Before you get to the last stanza with Tía Mónica moving all over, you can continue to add other parts of the body like the following:

las cejas	eyebrows
las pestañas	eyelashes
la nariz	nose
los codos	elbows
las manos	hands
las rodillas	knees

Book

There is so much you can do with a *rebozo*, and you can find out the many uses of this traditional Mexican woven shawl in the book that follows:

Tafolla, Carmen. *What Can You Do with a Rebozo?* Tricycle Press, 2008.

Song

This song has its tradition in Chile, and this fun version is by the musician José-Luis Orozco. Get the children on their feet so they can move freely as the song adds a body part with each verse.

JUANITO	LITTLE JOHNNY
Juanito cuando baila,	When little Johnny dances,
Baila, baila, baila.	He dances, dances, dances.
Juanito cuando baila,	When little Johnny dances,
Baila con el dedito,	He dances with his pinkie,

Con el dedito-ito-ito.	With his pinkie, pinkie, pinkie.
Así baila Juanito.	That's how Johnny dances.
Juanito cuando baila,	When little Johnny dances,
Baila, baila, baila.	He dances, dances, dances.
Juanito cuando baila,	When little Johnny dances,
Baila con el pie,	He dances with his foot,
Con el pie, pie, pie,	With his foot, foot, foot,
Con el dedito-ito-ito.	With his pinkie, pinkie, pinkie.
Así baila Juanito.	That's how Johnny dances.
Juanito cuando baila . . .	When little Johnny dances . . .
La rodilla-dilla-dilla . . .	Knee, knee, knee . . .
La cadera-dera-dera . . .	Hip, hip, hip . . .
La mano, mano, mano . . .	Hand, hand, hand . . .
El codo, codo, codo . . .	Elbow, elbow, elbow . . .
El hombro, hombro, hombro . . .	Shoulder, shoulder, shoulder . . .
La cabeza-eza-eza . . .	Head, head, head . . .

Book

This bilingual book can be read first in one language and then in the other. You may want to ask someone on staff or even one of your library customers to read the Spanish version while you read the English, or vice versa.

> Bertrand, Diane Gonzales. *We Are Cousins / Somos primos*. Piñata Books, 2007.

Song

Try singing this traditional song:

TIPITÍN	TIPITIN
Tipi tipi tin tipi tin.	Tipi tipi tin tipi tin.
Tipi tipi ton tipi ton.	Tipi tipi ton tipi ton.
Todas las mañanas	Every morning
Cuando me levanto	When I wake up
Canto esta canción.	I sing this song.

Tipi tipi tin tipi tin.	Tipi tipi tin tipi tin.
Tipi tipi ton tipi ton.	Tipi tipi ton tipi ton.
Todas las mañanas	Every morning
Cuando me levanto	When I wake up
Canto esta canción.	I sing this song.
Tipi tipi tin tipi tin.	Tipi tipi tin tipi tin.
Tipi tipi ton tipi ton.	Tipi tipi ton tipi ton.

Additional Books

This sampling of books includes good suggestions for parents to check out and read at home with their children:

> Amado, Elisa. *Cousins.* Groundwood Books, 2004. Spanish: *Primas.* Libros Tigrillos, 2003.
>
> Bernardo, Anilú. *A Day with My Aunts / Un día con mis tías.* Piñata Books, 2006.
>
> Cisneros, Sandra. *Hairs / Pelitos.* Knopf, 1997.
>
> Foster, Karen Sharp. *Good Night, My Little Chicks / Buenas noches, mis pollitos.* First Story Press, 1997.
>
> Sánchez, Mireia. *Sobre la arena.* Combel, 2000.

Closing Rhyme

You started your program with a rhyme, and you can end with the same rhyme or try something different.

PROGRAM 7: FESTIVALS AND FIESTAS / *LOS FESTIVALES Y LAS FIESTAS*

Opening Rhyme

Start your program with your opening rhyme.

Book

For this first book, you may want to purchase a piñata or even ask if any of your storytime parents might have one to share at storytime. Talk to your preschoolers about the piñata and how it is traditional at Latino birthday parties. If you have an outside area, consider having a piñata filled with candy and letting each child have a turn at hitting it. Be sure to have enough adult supervision and go over some rules to avoid bumps and bruises. You may want to rope off an area that kids cannot cross until the person hitting the piñata has the blindfold removed.

> Domínguez, Kelli Kyle. *The Perfect Piñata / La piñata perfecta*. Albert Whitman, 2002.

Song

Try singing or reciting one of the following traditional songs with the group:

BAJEN LA PIÑATA
Bajen la piñata,
Bájenla un tantito
Que le den de palos
Poquito a poquito.

LOWER THE PIÑATA
Lower the piñata,
Lower it a bit,
So that we can hit it
Bit by little bit.

LA PIÑATA
Dale, dale, dale,
No pierdas el tino.
Porque si lo pierdes
Pierdes el camino.

THE PIÑATA
Strike it, strike it, strike it,
Don't lose your grip.
Because if you lose it,
You will lose your way.

Book

Carnival, or *carnaval* in Spanish, is a special celebration held in some Latin American countries. Here's a book to share that is available in Spanish and in English:

> Delacre, Lulu. *Rafi and Rosi: Carnival!* Rayo, 2008. Spanish: *Rafi y Rosi: ¡Carnaval!* Rayo, 2006.

Game

This is a circle game where children pass a stick around the circle. The stick is used to keep the beat. The last person holding the stick (on the last word, *tran*) is out.

FANDANGO
Al son de un fandango,
   tango, tango
Cantaré.
Cantaré con alegría, y con
   el triqui

FANDANGO
With the sound of a fandango,
   tango, tango
I will sing.
I will sing with happiness, with
   the triqui

Triqui tran,
Con el triqui triqui tran.

Triqui tran,
With the triqui triqui tran.

Book

Birthdays are special for everyone. This book has a new twist and is available in Spanish and in English:

Lopez, Loretta. *Birthday Swap*. Lee and Low Books, 1997. Spanish: *¡Qué sorpresa de cumpleaños!* Lee and Low Books, 1997.

Song

This is a traditional Mexican birthday song:

LAS MAÑANITAS
Estas son las mañanitas
Que cantaba el rey David.
Hoy por ser día de tu santo
Te las cantamos a ti.

MEXICAN BIRTHDAY SONG
This is the morning
That King David sang about.
It is your saint's day
And we sing it for you.

Despierta, mi bien, despierta.
Mira que ya amaneció
Ya los pajaritos cantan;
La luna ya se metió.

Wake up, my dear, wake up.
Look, it's morning
And the birds are singing;
The moon has set.

Que linda está la mañana
En que vengo a saludarte.
Venimos todos con gusto
Y placer a felicitarte.

It's such a beautiful morning
And I come to greet you.
We come with great cheer
And joy to congratulate you.

Ya viene amaneciendo,
Ya la luz del día nos dio.
Levántate de mañana,
Mira que ya amaneció.

And now morning is here
And with it the light of day.
Get up on this fine morning,
You are awake now, my dear.

Additional Books

These are titles that you can easily share with parents:

Kleven, Elisa. *Hooray, a Piñata!* Penguin, 2000. Spanish: *¡Viva! ¡Una piñata!* Penguin Young Readers Group, 1996.

Levy, Janice. *Celebrate! It's Cinco de Mayo! / ¡Celebremos! Es el cinco de mayo!* Albert Whitman, 2007.

Torres, Leyla. *Kite Festival.* Farrar, Straus, and Giroux, 2004. Spanish: *El festival de cometas.* Farrar, Straus, and Giroux, 2004.

Closing Rhyme

You started your program with a rhyme, and you can end with the same rhyme or try something different.

PROGRAM 8: LETTERS AND WORDS / *LAS LETRAS Y PALABRAS*

Opening Rhyme

Start your program with your opening rhyme.

Alphabet Sounds

You can show the letters of the alphabet and sound them out in Spanish and in English. They look the same but sound different. Here are the pronunciations and sounds for the vowels in Spanish:

VOWEL	SPANISH	SOUND
A, a	a	ah
E, e	e	eh
I, i	i	ee
O, o	o	oh
U, u	u	ooh

Here are the pronunciations and sounds for the consonants in Spanish:

CONSONANT	SPANISH	SOUND
B, b	be	beh
C, c	ce	the *c* in *ce* and *ci* sounds like *s*, and in *ca*, *co*, and *cu* like *k*
D, d	de	deh
F, f	efe	feh
G, g	ge	the *g* in *ge* and *gi* sounds like "heh," and in *ga*, *go*, and *gu* like "geh"

H, h	hache	*h* is silent
J, j	jota	*j* sounds like *h*
K, k	ca	kah
L, l	ele	leh
M, m	eme	meh
N, n	ene	neh
Ñ, ñ	eñe	ñeh
P, p	pe	peh
Q, q	cu	coo
R, r	ere	roh
RR, rr	erre	roll your *r*'s
S, s	ese	seh
T, t	te	teh
V, v	ve	sounds like *b*
W, w	doble ve	wuh
X, x	equis	sounds like *h* in *he* (*México*) or like "ks" in *ax* (*éxito*)
Y, y	i griega	yeh
Z, z	zeta	sounds like *s*

The following are no longer recognized as individual letters of the Spanish alphabet:

| Ch | che | cheh |
| Ll | elle | ehyeh |

Book

Tabor, Nancy. *Albertina Goes Up: An Alphabet Book / Albertina anda arriba: El abecedario*. Charlesbridge, 1992.

Song

Now sing this song, or try it as a call-and-response chant. With each vowel, you are changing each verse.

LA MAR ESTABA SERENA
La mar estaba serena,
Serena estaba la mar.

THE SEA WAS SERENE
The sea was serene,
Serene was the sea.

A	A
La mar astaba sarana,	Tha saa was sarana,
Sarana astaba la mar.	Sarana was tha saa.
E	E
Le mer estebe serene,	The see wes serene,
Serene estebe le mer.	Serene wes the see.
I	I
Li mir istibi sirini,	Thi sii wis sirini,
Sirini istibi li mir.	Sirini wis thi sii.
O	O
Lo mor ostobo sorono,	Tho soo wos sorono,
Sorono ostobo lo mor.	Sorono wos tho soo.
U	U
Lu mur ustubu surunu,	Thu suu wus surunu,
Surunu ustubu lu mur.	Surunu wus thu suu.

Book

Although the following book is available only in Spanish, you'll be able to go over it page by page in English. Try it next and then ask your storytime group to tell you what their favorite letter is.

Robleda, Margarita. *Mis letras favoritas.* Ediciones Destino, 2003.

Or you might try this alphabet adventure:

Vargo, Sharon. *Señor Felipe's Alphabet Adventure: El alfabeto español.* Millbrook Press, 2000.

Song

Next, sing this traditional song about the vowels:

MARCHA DE LAS LETRAS	MARCH OF THE LETTERS
¡Que dejen toditos	Everyone
Los libros abiertos	Open your books
Ha sido la orden	By order
Que dio el general.	Of the general.

¡Que todos los niños	All children
Estén muy atentos,	Come to attention,
Las cinco vocales	The five vowels
Van a desfilar!	Are going to form a line!
Primero verás	First you'll see
Que pasa la *A*	The letter *A*
Con sus dos patitas	With two little legs
Muy abiertas al marchar.	Marching apart.
Ahí viene la *E*	Next comes *E*
Alzando los pies.	Picking up his feet.
El palo de en medio	The middle
Es más chico como ves.	Is much smaller, can't you see?
Aquí está la *I*,	Here is *I*,
Le sigue la *O*.	Then follows *O*.
Una es flaca y la otra	One is skinny and the other
Gorda porque ya comió.	Is fat because it just ate.
Y luego hasta atrás	Following behind
Llegó la *U*,	Enters *U*,
Como la cuerda	Like a rope
Con que siempre saltas tú.	That you'll jump through.

Additional Books

Use these titles on your display table for parents to check out and read to their children:

Ada, Alma Flor. *Abecedario de los animales*. Espasa-Calpe, 1998.

Avalos, Cecilia. *La fiesta del abecedario*. Sundance, 1993.

Perea Estrada, Altamira. *Un abecedario muy sabroso*. Scholastic, 1996.

Closing Rhyme

You started your program with a rhyme, and you can end with the same rhyme or try something different.

Chapter 5

PROGRAMS FOR SCHOOL-AGE CHILDREN
PROGRAMAS PARA NIÑOS DE PRIMARIA

Children in grade school are becoming more independent. They can use scissors, trace patterns, color, follow a rhythm pattern, follow instructions, repeat phrases, engage in group activities, and much more. They can also be a very excitable group, so ground rules should be set early.

Find a song, tongue twister, rhyme, or movement activity to open each of your programs. Here is a tongue-twister suggestion:

Me dicen que he dicho un dicho,	Someone said I said a saying,
A que dicho he dicho yo;	Said a saying so said I;
Este dicho está muy bien dicho	Such a saying so well said
Por haberlo dicho yo.	Seeing how I said it so.

PROGRAM 1: GRANDPARENTS / *LOS ABUELOS*

Opening Activity

Start your program with your opening welcome rhyme or song or movement activity. Then read a book together.

Book

> Ada, Alma Flor. *I Love Saturdays y Domingos*. Atheneum Books for Young Readers, 2002.

Song

This song is a traditional tune that you can teach your group. Ask the children to form a circle and hold hands or link arms together. They will be swaying left and right as they sing with you. You can find the song on some of the CDs listed in the discography.

DE COLORES	COLORS
De colores,	Oh, the colors!
De colores se visten los campos	The fields become colorfully dressed
En la primavera.	In springtime.
De colores,	Oh, the colors!
De colores son los pajaritos que	The birds that come from afar
Vienen de afuera.	Are so colorful.
De colores,	Oh, the colors!
De colores es el arco iris que	The rainbow that we see glowing
vemos lucir.	is colorful.
Y por eso los grandes amores	That's why I like this colorful
de muchos	world
Colores me gustan a mí.	So much.
Canta el gallo,	The rooster sings,
Canta el gallo con el	The rooster sings
Kiri, kiri, kiri, kiri, kiri.	Cock-a-doodle-doo.
La gallina,	The hen,
La gallina canta con el	The hen sings
Cara, cara, cara, cara, cara.	Cluck, cluck, cluck, cluck, cluck.
Los pollitos,	The chicks,
Los pollitos con el pío, pío,	The chicks sing cheep, cheep,
pío, pío, pí.	cheep, cheep, cheep.
Y por eso los grandes amores	That's why I like this colorful
de muchos	world
Colores me gustan a mí.	So much.

Book

Here is another book to share:

Costales, Amy. *Abuelita Full of Life / Abuelita, llena de vida*. Luna Rising, 2007.

Song

This is a favorite traditional song for you to sing with your group:

ARROZ CON LECHE	RICE WITH MILK
Arroz con leche,	Rice with milk,
Me quiero casar	I want to marry
Con una señorita	A young woman
De este lugar,	From this place.
Que sepa coser,	She must know how to sew,
Que sepa bordar,	She must know how to embroider,
Que sepa la tabla	She must know her
De multiplicar.	Multiplication tables.

Book

Carmen Lomas Garza is an award-winning author and artist, and she has several books that you can choose from. You can select certain sections from her books or read this one:

> Lomas Garza, Carmen. *In My Family / En mi familia.* Children's Book Press, 1996.

Craft: *Papel Picado*

Try this craft made with tissue paper. It is best done with an older group of school-age children, and you will want to set rules about safety with the scissors. You will also want to have parent volunteers to assist. *Papel picado* is a traditional art in some Latin American countries. These paper streamers with decorative cutouts are sometimes quite elaborate. They are often used at celebrations like birthday parties and holiday events.

> You will need:
> tissue paper
> scissors
>
> Instructions:
> 1. Distribute scissors and one sheet of tissue paper about the size of a sheet of construction paper (nine-by-eleven inches).
> 2. Fold the tissue paper into an accordion.
> 3. Use the scissors to clip geometric designs on each side of the paper.
> 4. Unfold the paper to see the shapes you have cut.

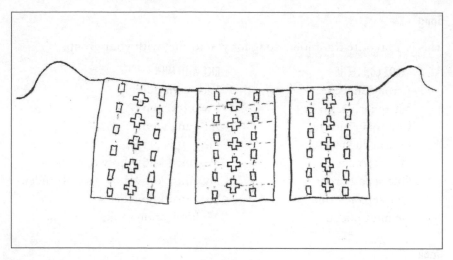

Papel picado

Additional Books

This is a list of books that you may want to recommend to children:

Castañeda, Omar S. *Abuela's Weave*. Lee and Low Books, 1995.
Spanish: *El tapiz de abuela*. Lee and Low Books, 1993.

Dorros, Arthur. *Abuela*. Dutton, 1991. Spanish: *Abuela*. Dutton, 1995.

Herrera, Juan Felipe. *Grandma and Me at the Flea / Los meros meros remateros*. Children's Book Press, 2002.

Luenn, Nancy. *A Gift for Abuelita: Celebrating the Day of the Dead / Un regalo para abuelita: En celebración del día de los muertos*. Rising Moon, 1998.

Nodar, Carmen Santiago. *Abuelita's Paradise*. A. Whitman, 1992. Spanish: *El paraíso de abuelita*. A. Whitman, 1992.

Torres, Leyla. *Liliana's Grandmothers / Las abuelas de Liliana*. Farrar, Straus, and Giroux, 1998.

Velasquez, Eric. *Grandma's Records*. Walker, 2001. Spanish: *Los discos de mi abuela*. Lectorum Publications, 2002.

Closing Activity

End your program with a rhyme or song or movement activity.

PROGRAM 2: BIRDS / *LOS AVES*

Opening Activity

Start your program with your opening welcome rhyme or song or movement activity. Then read a book together.

Book

Ada, Alma Flor. *Half-Chicken / Medio pollito*. Doubleday, 1997.

Craft: *Mola*

You will need to allow enough time to do this craft, and adult supervision is advised, so ask for teen or parent volunteers. *Molas* are made by tracing a design only once and then gluing it to another sheet of different-colored paper. The second sheet is cut around the first design, leaving a border so that you can see the second color. This is then glued to the third piece of paper and again cut, leaving a border so that you can now see all three colors of paper. The top color is the only one where you can see the entire design in that color. The other two colors become borders.

You will need:
patterns of different animals in three different sizes
    (e.g., fish, lizard, bird, turtle)
construction paper in different colors
pencil
scissors
glue

Instructions:

1. Select a pattern of one animal. Take all three sizes of that animal pattern.
2. Trace the smallest pattern on one sheet of construction paper. This will be the top of the *mola*.
3. Trace the next size pattern on a different color of construction paper.
4. Trace the biggest pattern on a different color of construction paper.
5. Cut out all three patterns that you have traced on the three different sheets of construction paper.
6. The smallest size will be the top. Glue this to the medium size.

7. Now glue the medium size to the largest size.
8. You have a *mola* made up of three different colors and sizes of the same animal.
9. You can use leftover scraps to add designs or facial features to your creatures.

Book

If you decide to do a craft with your program, you may want to limit the number of books you read. If time permits, here is a delightful story about a hen named Rosaura who wants only a bicycle for her birthday. Find out what happens when she gets her wish!

> Barbot, Daniel. *A Bicycle for Rosaura*. Kane/Miller, 1994. Spanish: *Rosaura en bicicleta*. Sagebrush Education Resources, 1992.

Motion Rhyme

Here is a motion rhyme about two little birds. Hold up two fingers and show them seated on your arm. Fly them away by bringing first one hand and then the other behind your back. Use a hand motion beckoning them to come back.

Dos pajaritos muy sentaditos,	Two little birds
En una cerca muy quietecitos.	Seated on a high fence.
Vuela Panchito, vuela Pedrito.	Fly Panchito, fly Pedrito.
Vuelve Panchito, vuelve Pedrito.	Come back Panchito, come back Pedrito.

Book

A traditional story about a rooster has been retold in the following bilingual edition. You will be the best judge as to whether time remains to include another story.

> González, Lucía M. *The Bossy Gallito: A Traditional Cuban Folktale / El gallo de bodas*. Scholastic, 1994.

Game

This is a traditional circle game, and there is no limit to the number of players. The words can be sung or chanted.

1. Choose a Doña Blanca and a *jicotillo* (hornet). Doña Blanca stands inside the circle and the *jicotillo* remains on the outside.
2. Children join hands and circle around Doña Blanca as they sing or chant. After the second verse, the *jicotillo* tries to break through clasped hands to catch Doña Blanca.
3. When the *jicotillo* succeeds in entering the circle, he or she chases Doña Blanca. Doña Blanca cannot run outside of the circle.
4. When she has been caught, Doña Blanca chooses a new *jicotillo* before she becomes part of the circle. The old *jicotillo* is now the new Doña Blanca.

DOÑA BLANCA
Doña Blanca está cubierta
Con pilares de oro y plata.
Romperemos un pilar
Para ver a Doña Blanca.

¿Quién es ese jicotillo
Que anda en pos de Doña Blanca?
¡Yo soy ése, yo soy ése
Que anda en pos de Doña Blanca!

DOÑA BLANCA
Doña Blanca all surrounded
By pillars of silver and gold.
Break a column now
If Doña Blanca you will hold.

Who is this hornet
Who chases Doña Blanca?

I am he, I am he
Who's trying to catch her!

Additional Books

Use these books during visits in the classroom or as books to display to encourage checking them out:

Ada, Alma Flor. *The Rooster Who Went to His Uncle's Wedding: A Latin American Folktale*. Putnam, 1993. Spanish: *El gallo que fue a la boda de su tío: Cuento popular hispanoamericano*. Putnam and Grosset Group, 1998.

López de Mariscal, Blanca. *The Harvest Birds / Los pájaros de la cosecha*. Children's Book Press, 1995.

Madrigal, Antonio Hernández. *Blanca's Feather / La pluma de Blanca*. Rising Moon, 2001.

Closing Activity

End your program with a rhyme or song or movement activity.

PROGRAM 3: SOUP, TORTILLAS, AND MEXICAN FOOD / *CALDO, TORTILLAS Y COMIDAS MEXICANAS*

Opening Activity

Start your program with your opening welcome rhyme or song or movement activity.

Book

Next, read this book about two young girls who decide to save a rooster when they find out that he is meant to be dinner!

De Anda, Diane. *Quiquiriquí / Kikirikí*. Piñata Books, 2004.

Song

Next, sing this traditional song about a sickly donkey:

A MI BURRO, A MI BURRO	MY DONKEY, MY DONKEY
A mi burro, a mi burro,	My donkey, my donkey,
Le duele la cabeza,	His head hurts,
El médico le ha puesto	So the doctor has given him
Una gorrita negra,	A black bonnet,
Una gorrita negra.	A black bonnet.
A mi burro, a mi burro,	My donkey, my donkey,
Le duele la garganta,	His throat hurts,
El médico le ha puesto	So the doctor has given him
Una corbata blanca,	A white necktie,
Una corbata blanca,	A white necktie,
Una gorrita negra.	A black bonnet.
A mi burro, a mi burro,	My donkey, my donkey,
Le duele la nariz,	His nose hurts,
El médico le ha puesto	So the doctor has given him
Agüita con anís,	Water with anise,
Agüita con anís,	Water with anise,
Una corbata blanca,	A white necktie,
Una gorrita negra.	A black bonnet.
A mi burro, a mi burro,	My donkey, my donkey,
Le duele el corazón,	His heart hurts,

El médico le ha dado	So the doctor has given him
Jarabe de limón,	Little drops of lemon,
Jarabe de limón,	Little drops of lemon,
Agüita con anís,	Water with anise,
Una corbata blanca,	A white necktie,
Una gorrita negra.	A black bonnet.

A mi burro, a mi burro	My donkey, my donkey,
Ya no le duele nada.	Nothing hurts him now.
Pero el muy perezoso,	But now he's very lazy,
Durmiendo está en la cama.	He's sleeping in my bed.

Book

Magda is learning to make tortillas in this bilingual book:

> Chavarría-Cháirez, Becky. *Magda's Tortillas / Las tortillas de Magda*.
> Piñata Books, 2000.

Rhyme

Start this activity by talking about tortillas; you might even show pictures of tortillas. Start clapping, hand over hand, showing the motion of tortillas being prepared for cooking.

TORTILLITAS	LITTLE TORTILLAS
Tortillitas para mamá.	Little tortillas for Mommy.
Tortillitas para papá.	Little tortillas for Daddy.
Las quemaditas para mamá.	Toasty burnt ones for Mommy.
Las bonitas para papá.	Perfect round ones for Daddy.

Do this again, this time giving Mamá the perfect round ones.

Tortillitas para papá.	Little tortillas for Daddy.
Tortillitas para mamá.	Little tortillas for Mommy.
Las quemaditas para papá.	Toasty burnt ones for Daddy.
Las bonitas para mamá.	Perfect round ones for Mommy.

Book

Read this book, which is available in Spanish and in English, about a birthday celebration with some help with preparations from some sneaky little mice:

> Ryan, Pam Muñoz. *Mice and Beans*. Scholastic, 2001. Spanish: *Arroz con frijoles y unos amables ratones*. Scholastic, 2001.

Song

Here's a song about the days of the week and what's to eat on each day. You can sing it to the tune of "Frère Jacques." It was adapted by a children's librarian named Irene González.

Hoy es lunes.	Today is Monday.
Hoy es lunes.	Today is Monday.
¿Qué comer?	What's to eat?
¿Qué comer?	What's to eat?
Lunes los ejotes.	Monday, string beans.
Lunes los ejotes.	Monday, string beans.
Mmm, mmm, mmm.	Mmm, mmm, mmm.
Hoy es martes.	Today is Tuesday.
Hoy es martes.	Today is Tuesday.
¿Qué comer?	What's to eat?
¿Qué comer?	What's to eat?
Martes los camotes.	Tuesday, sweet potatoes.
Lunes los ejotes,	Monday, green beans.
Mmm, mmm, mmm.	Mmm, mmm, mmm.
Hoy es miércoles.	Today is Wednesday.
Hoy es miércoles.	Today is Wednesday.
¿Qué comer?	What's to eat?
¿Qué comer?	What's to eat?
Miércoles las fresas.	Wednesday, strawberries.
Martes los camotes.	Tuesday, sweet potatoes.
Lunes los ejotes.	Monday, green beans.
Mmm, mmm, mmm.	Mmm, mmm, mmm.
Hoy es jueves.	Today is Thursday.
Hoy es jueves.	Today is Thursday.
¿Qué comer?	What's to eat?
¿Qué comer?	What's to eat?
Jueves las cerezas.	Thursday, cherries.
Miércoles las fresas.	Wednesday, strawberries.
Martes los camotes.	Tuesday, sweet potatoes.
Lunes los ejotes.	Monday, green beans.
Mmm, mmm, mmm.	Mmm, mmm, mmm.

Hoy es viernes.	Today is Friday.
Hoy es viernes.	Today is Friday.
¿Qué comer?	What's to eat?
¿Qué comer?	What's to eat?
Viernes el pescado.	Friday, fish.
Jueves las cerezas.	Thursday, cherries.
Miércoles las fresas.	Wednesday, strawberries.
Martes los camotes.	Tuesday, sweet potatoes.
Lunes los ejotes.	Monday, green beans.
Mmm, mmm, mmm.	Mmm, mmm, mmm.
Hoy es sábado.	Today is Saturday.
Hoy es sábado.	Today is Saturday.
¿Qué comer?	What's to eat?
¿Qué comer?	What's to eat?
Sábado, helado.	Saturday, ice cream.
Viernes el pescado.	Friday, fish.
Jueves las cerezas.	Thursday, cherries.
Miércoles las fresas.	Wednesday, strawberries.
Martes los camotes.	Tuesday, sweet potatoes.
Lunes los ejotes.	Monday, green beans.
Mmm, mmm, mmm.	Mmm, mmm, mmm.
Hoy es domingo.	Today is Sunday.
Hoy es domingo.	Today is Sunday.
¿Qué comer?	What's to eat?
¿Qué comer?	What's to eat?
Domingo, como todo.	Sunday, I eat everything.
Sábado, helado.	Saturday, ice cream.
Viernes el pescado.	Friday, fish.
Jueves las cerezas.	Thursday, cherries.
Miércoles las fresas.	Wednesday, strawberries.
Martes los camotes.	Tuesday, sweet potatoes.
Lunes los ejotes.	Monday, green beans.
¡Ay de mí! ¡Ay de mí!	My, oh my! My, oh my!

Additional Books

Here are some suggestions for more books to share. Hand these to your school-age children:

Baca, Ana. *Benito's Sopaipillas / Las sopaipillas de Benito*. Piñata Books, 2006.

Baca, Ana. *Chiles for Benito / Chiles para Benito*. Piñata Books, 2003.

Bertrand, Diane Gonzales. *Sip, Slurp, Soup, Soup / Caldo, caldo, caldo*. Piñata Books, 1997.

Mora, Pat. *The Bakery Lady / La señora de la panadería*. Piñata Books, 2001.

Tabor, Nancy Maria Grande. *A Taste of the Mexican Market / El gusto del mercado mexicano*. Charlesbridge, 1996.

Zepeda, Gwendolyn. *Growing Up with Tamales / Los tamales de Ana*. Piñata Books, 2008.

Closing Activity

End your program with a rhyme or song or movement activity.

PROGRAM 4: GHOSTS, SKELETONS, AND THE BOGEYMAN / *ESPANTOS, CALAVERAS Y EL CUCÚY*

Opening Activity

Start your program with your opening welcome rhyme or song or movement activity. Then read a book together.

Book

This book is available only in Spanish, but don't let that stop you. It is a classic and soon you will have your entire group chanting, "Chumba la cachumba, la cachumbabá."

Cotte, Carlos. *Chumba la cachumba*. Ediciones Ekaré, 1995.

Craft: Mexican Tissue Flowers

Day of the Dead, or *día de los muertos,* is a celebration of those who have died. Death is not feared in the Latino culture but rather celebrated. You might want to have a display of the altar that is designed for those loved ones who have died. Often, tissue flowers decorate the altar or *ofrenda,* as it is called in Spanish.

Here is a craft activity that you can do with your group. It is best to have the tissue paper precut into the five-inch-by-five-inch squares.

You will need:
tissue paper in assorted colors
chenille stems or pipe cleaners (two per person)

Instructions:
1. Cut the tissue paper into five-inch-by-five-inch squares.
2. Distribute four squares of tissue paper in various colors to each child.
3. Distribute two chenille stems per person.
4. With the four tissue squares together, make an accordion.
5. Keep the accordion in place by taking one chenille stem and twisting the top over the middle part of the tissue paper accordion.
6. Separate the tissue paper by lifting and fluffing up one at a time to give the appearance of a flower in bloom.
7. Twist the top layer to form the center of the flower.
8. Use the other chenille stem to make the leaves on the stem.

Book

Señor Calavera has come knocking, but he is in for a surprise in this English-language book with Spanish words sprinkled throughout:

> Morales, Yuyi. *Just a Minute: A Trickster Tale and Counting Book*. Chronicle Books, 2003.

Craft: *Calavera Mask*

You may want to do a craft activity with the group, and you can make a skull or *calavera* mask or make a skeleton puppet. Patterns for both are included here.

You will need:
calavera mask pattern (see p. 95)
crayons and/or markers
hole punch
yarn
scissors

Instructions:
1. Distribute *calavera* mask pattern and crayons or markers.
2. Children color in their mask.

3. When finished, cut out the mask.
4. Punch a hole on each side of the mask.
5. Tie yarn through each hole so the mask can be tied around each child's head.

Craft: Skeleton Puppet

You will need:
skeleton puppet parts (see p. 96)
scissors
brads
thin wooden dowels or straws
tape

Instructions:

1. Cut out the skeleton parts.
2. Secure the parts with the metal brads.
3. Tape the skeleton puppet to the wooden dowel or straw.

Tongue Twister

Here is a tongue twister to try with the group:

El pelo al codo	From hair to elbow
Y del codo al pelo.	And from elbow to hair.
Del codo al pelo	From elbow to hair
Y del pelo al codo.	And from hair to elbow.

Additional Books

A few more scary tales follow. Children are sure to check them out if you share them in the classroom or display them in a prominent place in the library with good signage.

Anzaldúa, Gloria. *Prietita and the Ghost Woman / Prietita y La Llorona.* Children's Book Press, 1996.

Brusca, María Cristina. *The Blacksmith and the Devils.* Henry Holt, 1992. Spanish: *El herrero y el diablo.* Henry Holt, 1992.

Corpi, Lucha. *Where Fireflies Dance / Ahí, donde bailan las luciérnagas.* Children's Book Press, 1997.

Galindo, Claudia. *Do You Know the Cucuy? / ¿Conoces al cucuy?* Piñata Books, 2008.

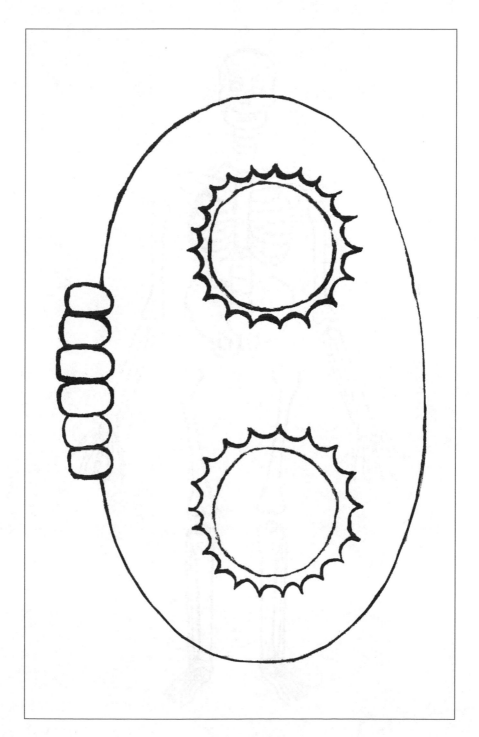

Calavera mask

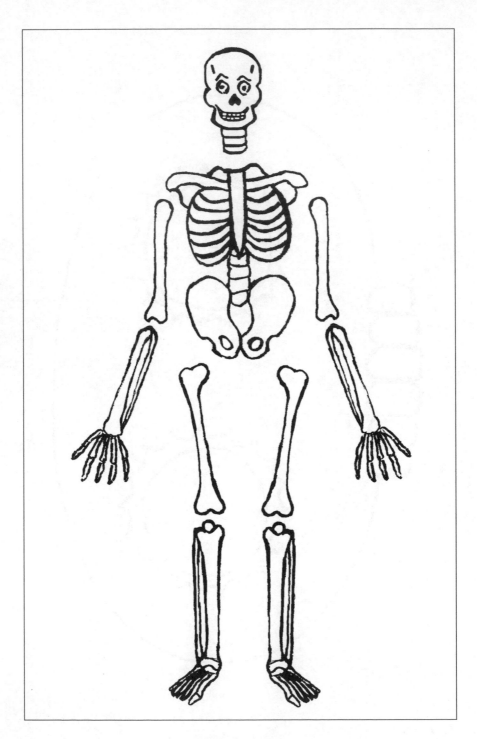

Skeleton puppet

González, Ada Acosta. *Mayte and the Bogeyman / Mayte y el cuco*.
Piñata Books, 2006.

Closing Activity

End your program with a rhyme or song or movement activity.

PROGRAM 5: MIGRANT WORKERS AND THE FAMILY / *CAMPESINOS Y LA FAMILIA*

Opening Activity

Start your program with your opening welcome rhyme or song or movement activity. Then read a book together.

Book

Tomás Rivera was the son of migrant workers. This is a story about him that is available in a Spanish and English edition. Rivera went on to be the first Mexican American to hold the position of chancellor at the University of California, Riverside.

Mora, Pat. *Tomás and the Library Lady*. Random House, 1997.
Spanish: *Tomás y la señora de la biblioteca*. Dragonfly Books, 1997.

Movement Activity

This movement activity is similar to the game "London Bridge":

1. Choose two children to be the "cave." They need to face each other, with their arms raised to allow the serpent to pass between them.
2. Line up the other children to form the serpent. They chant the words. At the phrase "Tras, tras, tras, tras!" the two children who are forming the cave drop their arms and catch the person who is between them.
3. The child who is caught takes the place as part of the cave, and one who was originally part of the cave joins the end of the serpent.

A LA VÍBORA DE LA MAR	THE SEA SERPENT
A la víbora, víbora de la mar, de la mar,	The serpent, serpent of the sea
Por aquí pueden pasar;	Can pass through here, through here;
Los de adelante corren mucho,	The ones in front run very fast,
Y los de atrás se quedarán.	Those in back get left behind.
¡Tras, tras, tras, tras!	Tras, tras, tras, tras!
Una mexicana,	A Mexican girl
Que fruta vendía—	Who sold fruit—
Ciruela, chabacano,	Plums or apricots,
Melón o sandía.	Cantaloupes or watermelons.
Verbena, verbena,	Verbena, verbena,
Jardín de matatena.	In a garden of jacks.
Verbena, verbena,	Verbena, verbena,
Jardín de matatena.	In a garden of jacks.
Campanita de oro,	Little bell of gold,
Déjame pasar	Let me pass
Con todos mis hijos,	With all my children,
¡Menos el de atrás!	Except the last!
¡Tras, tras, tras, tras!	Tras, tras, tras, tras!

Book

Before reading this book, you might want to talk a little about migrant workers and about how these seasonal workers often move depending on what crop needs to be picked.

> Pérez, L. King. *First Day in Grapes*. Lee and Low Books, 2002.
> Spanish: *Primer día en las uvas*. Lee and Low Books, 2004.

Craft: *Balero*

Here is a craft idea for making a toy called a *balero*. This toy is usually made of wood. A ball is attached by string to the *balero*. The object is to catch the ball in the cone.

You will need:
tagboard
markers or crayons
stapler
string
large round beads
hole punch
tape
reinforcements

Instructions:

1. Cut a piece of tagboard into a quarter circle. (This is going to be made into a cone.)
2. Decorate the outside of the cone with festive designs using markers and crayons.
3. Punch a hole in the middle of what will be the top of the cone, and adhere reinforcements to the inside and outside (the curved side).
4. Bring both ends of the cone together and staple the top and bottom tip of the cone.
5. Use tape to keep the sides together.
6. String a large bead onto the end of about a twelve-inch piece of string and tie in place.
7. Tie the other end of the string through the reinforced hole.

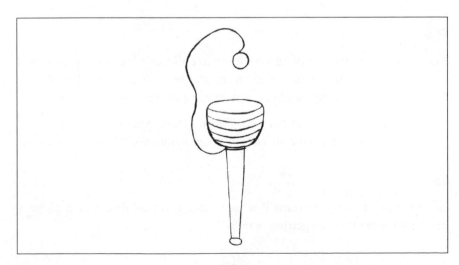

Balero

Additional Books

Here is a list of books for you to share with your group. Display them prominently and have children check them out:

> Ada, Alma Flor. *Gathering the Sun: An Alphabet in Spanish and English.* Lothrop, 1997.
>
> Altman, Linda Jacobs. *Amelia's Road.* Lee and Low Books, 1993. Spanish: *El camino de Amelia.* Lee and Low Books, 1993.
>
> Dorros, Arthur. *Radio Man / Don Radio.* Harper, 1993.
>
> Herrera, Juan Felipe. *Calling the Doves / El canto de las palomas.* Children's Book Press, 1995.
>
> Herrera, Juan Felipe. *The Upside-Down Boy / El niño de cabeza.* Children's Book Press, 2000.
>
> Jiménez, Francisco. *La mariposa.* Houghton Mifflin, 1998.

Closing Activity

End your program with a rhyme or song or movement activity.

PROGRAM 6: FOLKLORE / *FOLCLORE*

Opening Activity

Start your program with your opening welcome rhyme or song or movement activity.

Book

The Pura Belpré Award noting excellence in children's literature was named after the first Latina children's librarian at the New York Public Library. One of her folktales that she shared with her storytime group is this one:

> Belpré, Pura. *Pérez and Martina.* Warne, 1960. Spanish: *Pérez y Martina: Un cuento folklórico puertorriqueño.* Warne, 1966.

Song

After reading this story, you will want to sing this traditional song about a louse and a flea that are getting married!

EL PIOJO Y LA PULGA

El piojo y la pulga se van a
  casar.
No se han casado por falta
  de maíz.
Tiro lo tiro lo tiro liro
  liro,
Tiro lo tiro lo liro
  liro la.

Responde el gorgojo desde
  su maizal:
"Hágase la boda que yo doy
  el maíz."
Tiro lo tiro lo tiro
  liro liro,
Tiro lo tiro lo liro
  liro la.

Bendito sea el cielo que todo
  tenemos,
¿Pero los padrinos dónde
  agarraremos?
Tiro lo tiro lo tiro
  liro liro,
Tiro lo tiro lo tiro lo liro
  liro la.

Salta el ratón desde el ratonal:
"Amarren al gato que yo iré
  a apadrinar."
Tiro lo tiro lo tiro
  liro liro.
Tiro lo tiro lo liro
  liro la.

El piojo y la pulga se van
  a casar.
Les pregunta el padre si
  saben rezar.

THE LOUSE AND THE FLEA

The louse and the flea are getting
  married.
They haven't yet for lack
  of corn.
Deedle di, deedle do, diddle, liddle,
  liddle,
Deedle di, deedle do, diddle,
  liddle, la.

From the cornfield, the weevil
  replies:
"Have the wedding, I'll provide
  the corn."
Deedle di, deedle do, diddle,
  liddle, liddle,
Deedle di, deedle do, diddle,
  liddle, la.

Thanks to the sky for
  providing,
But where will we find the
  godparents?
Deedle di, deedle do, diddle,
  liddle, liddle,
Deedle di, deedle do, diddle,
  liddle, la.

Out jumps the mouse, who shouts:
"Tie up the cat and I'll be the
  godfather."
Deedle di, deedle do, diddle,
  liddle, liddle.
Deedle di, deedle do, diddle,
  liddle, la.

The louse and the flea are getting
  married.
The minister asks if they know
  how to pray.

Tiro lo tiro lo tiro liro liro,	Deedle di, deedle do, diddle, liddle, liddle,
Tiro lo tiro lo tiro lo liro liro la.	Deedle di, deedle do, diddle, liddle, la.
Salta la pulga que se desafina:	Out jumps a flea singing totally out of tune:
"Tráiganme unas naguas yo seré madrina."	"Bring me a petticoat and I'll be the godmother."
Tiro lo tiro lo tiro liro liro,	Deedle di, deedle do, diddle, liddle, liddle,
Tiro lo tiro lo liro liro la.	Deedle di, deedle do, diddle, liddle, la.
Se acabó la boda, hubo mucho vino	The wedding is over, there was lots of wine.
Se soltó el gatito y se comió al padrino.	The cat escaped and then he ate the godfather.
Tiro lo tiro lo tiro liro liro,	Deedle di, deedle do, diddle, liddle, liddle,
Tiro lo tiro lo liro liro la.	Deedle di, deedle do, diddle, liddle, la.
En la madrugada cuando el sol salió	In the early hours, when the sun began to rise,
No hubo ni un changuito que no se rascó.	There wasn't one left who didn't scratch his head.
Tiro lo tiro lo tiro liro liro,	Deedle di, deedle do, diddle, liddle, liddle,
Tiro lo tiro lo liro liro la.	Deedle di, deedle do, diddle, liddle, la.

Book

Pat Mora says she wrote this next book while thinking of Paul Bunyan and wondering about a similar character she might write about who was Bunyan's female counterpart:

> Mora, Pat. *Doña Flor: A Tall Tale about a Giant Woman with a Great Big Heart*. Knopf, 2005. Spanish: *Doña Flor: Un cuento de una mujer gigante con un grande corazón*. Dragonfly Books, 2005.

Game

Here is a simple game in which children kneel in a circle with their hands behind their back. One child is the leader while another is in the middle of the circle with his or her eyes closed. The leader goes around the outside of the circle and puts a small object into one child's hand. The person in the middle must guess who is holding the object.

El florón está en la mano	The flower is in the hand
Y en la mano está el florón.	And in the hand is the flower.
Adivina quien lo tiene	You must guess who has the flower
O te quedas de plantón.	Or you stay waiting in the circle.

Book

Here is a bilingual spin on the tale of Cinderella:

Hayes, Joe. *Little Gold Star / Estrellita de oro: A Cinderella Cuento.* Cinco Puntos Press, 2000.

Craft: Aztec Fan

This craft should be done with assistance from teens or adults so that the process goes smoothly.

You will need:
two small paper plates
tissue paper in assorted colors
construction paper
scissors
stapler
glue
wooden craft sticks
markers
crayons
feathers

Instructions:

1. Decorate one paper plate by first dividing it equally into several parts and drawing lines with markers or crayons.
2. Cut a small circle out of construction paper, which will go in the middle of the paper plate.
3. Draw an Aztec-inspired design or Aztec creature in the small circle. Some suggestions include a bird, the sun, or a snake.

4. Glue the decorated circle to the center of your top plate.
5. Fringe some tissue paper. You can fold a piece of tissue paper in the middle and fringe almost to the fold.
6. Glue the fringe to the inside of the top paper plate, gluing on the fold. You will have a double fringe.
7. Glue feathers on the paper plate.
8. Glue a craft stick to one end.
9. Glue or staple both paper plates together

Additional Books

Here are a few more folktales to talk about and encourage the children to check out:

Ehlert, Lois. *Cuckoo: A Mexican Folktale / Cucu: Un cuento folklórico mexicano*. Harcourt, 1997.

Ehlert, Lois. *Moon Rope: A Peruvian Folktale / Un lazo a la luna: Una leyenda peruana*. Harcourt Brace Jovanovich, 1992.

Hayes, Joe. *The Day It Snowed Tortillas: Tales from Spanish New Mexico*. Cinco Puntos Press, 2003.

Moretón, Daniel. *La Cucaracha Martina: A Caribbean Folktale*. Turtle Books, 1997. Spanish: *La cucaracha Martina: Un cuento folklórico del Caribe*. Turtle Books, 1997.

Villaseñor, Victor. *Mother Fox and the Coyote / Mamá Zorra y Don Coyote*. Piñata Books, 2004.

Closing Activity

End your program with a rhyme or song or movement activity.

PROGRAM 7: FAMOUS PEOPLE / *PERSONAS FAMOSAS*

Opening Activity

Start your program with your opening welcome rhyme or song or movement activity. Then read a book together.

Book

Andrews-Goebel, Nancy. *The Pot That Juan Built*. Lee and Low Books, 2002. Spanish: *La vasija que Juan fabricó*. Lee and Low Books, 2004.

Craft: Sun Face

After reading this story, you may want to try this craft. Be sure to provide adult supervision when your group is using scissors.

You will need:
paper plates
pencils
construction paper in different colors
markers or crayons
glue
scissors

Instructions:

1. Draw a sun design onto a paper plate.
2. Fold paper plate gently in half and cut out a mouth.
3. Cut out the sun design.
4. Cut out eyes, eyebrows, nose, and so on, from construction paper and attach with glue.
5. Decorate with markers or crayons.

Sun face

Book

Celia Cruz was a famous Cuban singer. You can share her life with your group via this bilingual book.

> Brown, Monica. *My Name Is Celia: The Life of Celia Cruz / Me llamo Celia: La vida de Celia Cruz.* Luna Rising, 2004.

Song

Try this song with your group:

TROMPO BAILARÍN	DANCING TOP
Baila que baila,	Dance, dance,
Mi caballero.	My gentleman.
Capa ceñida,	Fitted cape,
Punta de acero.	Steel tip.
Cuando tú bailas	When you dance
Florece el viento	The wind whirls up
En clavelitos	Just like spinning
Volatineros.	Carnations.
Zumba que zumba	Zumba, zumba,
Mi maromero.	my whirly top.
¡Que te mareas!	You'll get dizzy!
¡Remolinero!	You whirlpool!

Book

The award-winning team of Lucía González and Lulu Delacre have brought this book to us, which is a story of Pura Belpré, the first Latina children's librarian at the New York Public Library.

> González, Lucía. *The Storyteller's Candle / La velita de los cuentos.* Children's Book Press, 2008.

After reading this book, you may want to point out a display of other books by Pura Belpré. You may want to take one of her folktales and retell it as a puppet show or as a readers' theater presentation. A readers' theater presentation would give the leader an opportunity to assign parts to be read from a prepared script. Each participant reads part of the text, taking turns with other assigned readers.

Additional Books

Here are a few more books that you will want to promote at your library:

Benatar, Raquel. *Isabel Allende: Memories for a Story / Isabel Allende: Recuerdos para un cuento.* Piñata Books, 2004.

Bernier-Grand, Carmen T. *César: ¡Sí, se puede! Yes, We Can!* Marshall Cavendish, 2004.

Brown, Monica. *My Name Is Gabito: The life of Gabriel García Márquez / Me llamo Gabito: La vida de Gabriel García Márquez.* Luna Rising, 2007.

Griswold del Castillo, Richard. *César Chávez: The Struggle for Justice / César Chávez: La lucha por la justicia.* Piñata Books, 2008.

Krull, Kathleen. *Harvesting Hope: The Story of César Chávez.* Harcourt, 2003. Spanish: *Cosechando esperanza: La historia de César Chávez.* Harcourt, 2003.

Closing Activity

End your program with a rhyme or song or movement activity.

PROGRAM 8: POETRY / *POESÍA*

Opening Activity

Start your program with your opening welcome rhyme or song or movement activity. Then read selections from any of the following books.

Book

Alarcón, Francisco X. *Angels Ride Bikes and Other Fall Poems / Los ángeles andan en bicicleta y otros poemas de otoño.* Children's Book Press, 1999.

Alarcón, Francisco X. *Animal Poems of the Iguazú / Animalario del Iguazú.* Children's Book Press, 2008.

Alarcón, Francisco X. *From the Bellybutton of the Moon: And Other Summer Poems / Del ombligo de la luna: Y otros poemas de verano.* Children's Book Press, 2005.

Alarcón, Francisco X. *Iguanas in the Snow: And Other Winter Poems / Iguanas en la nieve: Y otros poemas de invierno.* Children's Book Press, 2005.

Alarcón, Francisco X. *Laughing Tomatoes and Other Spring Poems / Jitomates risueños y otros poemas de primavera*. San Francisco: Children's Book Press, 1997.

Mora, Pat. *Confetti: Poems for Children*. New York: Lee and Low Books, 1999.

Nye, Naomi Shihab. *The Tree Is Older Than You Are: A Bilingual Gathering of Poems and Stories from Mexico with Paintings by Mexican Artists*. Simon and Schuster, 1995.

Activity

After you share poetry with your group, you can engage in either of the following activities:

Make a bilingual poet tree. Distribute index cards to the children and ask them to write a simple poem. Punch a hole in the corner of the index card and hang the cards from a poem tree made from either a small potted tree in your library or a branch that you can hang from a good location in your library.

Have a poetry exchange. Have your group select their favorite poetry and ask them to read them out loud in Spanish and in English. Set up a stage and invite parents and teachers.

Rhyme

All rhymes are forms of poetry, so you can definitely engage your group in any of the countless rhymes you find in books. You can sing this traditional song, and you can find different versions on various CDs found in the discography:

LOS DIEZ PERRITOS	TEN PUPPIES
Yo tenía diez perritos,	I had ten puppies,
Uno se perdió en la nieve;	One got lost in the snow;
Ya no más me quedan nueve.	Now I only have nine.
De los nueve que quedaban,	Of the nine I had left,
Uno se comió un bizcocho;	One ate a biscuit;
Ya no más me quedan ocho.	Now I only have eight.
De los ocho que quedaban,	Of the eight I had left,
Uno fue por un juguete;	One left to find a toy;
Ya no más me quedan siete.	Now I only have seven.

De los siete que quedaban,	Of the seven I had left,
Uno se quemó los pies;	One burned his paws;
Ya no más me quedan seis.	Now I only have six.
De los seis que quedaban,	Of the six I had left,
Uno se fue brinco y brinco;	One jumped away;
Ya no más me quedan cinco.	Now I only have five.
De los cinco que quedaban,	Of the five I had left,
Uno se marcho al teatro;	One marched off to the theater;
Ya no más me quedan cuatro.	Now I only have four.
De los cuatro que quedaban,	Of the four I had left,
Uno se volteó al revés;	One turned backward;
Ya no más me quedan tres.	Now I only have three.
De los tres que quedaban,	Of the three I had left,
Uno fue a comprar arroz;	One left to buy rice;
Ya no más me quedan dos.	Now I only have two.
De los dos que quedaban,	Of the two I had left,
Uno se murió de ayuno;	One died of starvation;
Ya no más me queda uno.	Now I only have one.
Este uno que quedaba,	Of the one I had left,
Se lo llevó mi cuñada;	My sister-in-law took one;
Ya no me queda nada.	Now I don't have any.
Cuando ya no tenía nada,	And when I didn't have any,
La perra crió otra vez;	My dog conceived again;
Y ahora tengo otros	And now once again, I have ten
diez.	puppies.

Closing Activity

End your program with a rhyme or song or movement activity.

CONCLUSION

By now, you have encountered a variety of programs that reach out to children of different ages. Try a few and you will eventually see what works best with your group and your style of presentation. Use music CDs such as those suggested in the discography, and consider inviting outside presenters on occasion.

The intent of this book is to provide librarians and educators with ideas to implement bilingual programs for children. As with all storytime programs, it is very important to examine all books carefully and select only those that you love. Practice in advance, and if you do not speak Spanish or are not sure of pronunciation, ask for help from a teacher, a parent, or a coworker.

For those of us who are comfortable and familiar with books published in the United States, it may be easy to make a judgment about books published in other countries. Perhaps the binding is not what you are used to and the illustrations seem exaggerated or cartoonlike. What works and is even award-winning art for some may not have the same effect on others.

Standards also vary. Good binding in Mexico may not seem so to some here. The resources in the United States are abundant. That is not always the case in other countries. Although we know this, it is very easy to forget when we examine children's books. You might pass up a really good story that kids will enjoy and cherish. Children learn to value what we teach them has value, so have fun with your groups and don't be afraid to try new things!

PROGRAMS AT A GLANCE

This appendix provides brief lists of the contents of each program in the book. If no specific title is given for part of a program, I've left the choice to you. Songs and rhymes are identified by first lines when titles are not given.

CHAPTER 2

Program 1: The Alphabet / *El alfabeto*

Opening Song: "Hola, bebé / Hello, Baby"
Book: *The Alphabet / El alfabeto* by Gladys Rosa-Mendoza
Tickle Rhyme: "A, E, I, O, U."
Book: *Jugando con las vocales* by Margarita Robleda
Fingerplay: "A, el burro se va. / A, there goes the donkey."
Call-and-Response Rhyme: "Las cinco vocales son / The five vowels are"
Book: *A Is for Alphabet / A de alfabeto* by Michele Salas
Rhyme: "Vocales / Vowels"
Additional Books
Closing Song: "Adios, bebé / Good-bye, baby"

Program 2: Baby Animals / *Los animalitos*

Opening Song: "Hola, bebé / Hello, Baby"
Vocabulary Activity: "La vaca dice muu. / The cow says moo."
Book: *Five Little Ducks / Los cinco patitos* by Pamela Paparone
Rhyme: "El pato / The Duck"
Book: *Here, Kitty, Kitty! / ¡Ven, gatita, ven!* by Pat Mora
Rhyme: "Arre, borriquito / Giddyup, Little Burro"

Book: *Piggies / Cerditos* by Audrey Wood
Fingerplay: "Los cochinitos / The Little Pigs"
Clapping Rhyme: "Palmitas / Let's Clap" or "Tilín, tilín / Trot, Trot"
Additional Books
Closing Song: "Adios, bebé / Good-bye, Baby" or "Los pollitos / Baby
    Chicks"

Program 3: Babies / *Los bebés*

Opening Activity
Fingerplay: "Este chiquito es mi hermanito. / This tiny one is my little
    brother."
Book: *Baby! Baby!* by Vicky Ceelen
Rhyme: "Pon, pon, tata, / Pon, pon, la, la,"
Book: *Where Is Baby's Belly Button? / ¿Dónde está el ombliguito?* by
    Karen Katz
Song: "Debajo de un botón-tón-tón, / Underneath a button-ton-ton,"
Tickle Rhyme: "Tú padre ha venido. / Here comes Daddy."
Book: *Hugs and Kisses / Besitos y abrazos* by Roberta Grobel Intrater
Motion Rhyme: "El día en que tú naciste / On the Day You Were
    Born"
Additional Books
Closing Activity

Program 4: Food / *La comida*

Opening Activity
Vocabulary Activity: "la manzana / apple"
Book: *Let's Eat! / ¡A comer!* by Pat Mora
Clapping Rhyme: "Papas / Potatoes"
Book: *Eat! / ¡Qué rico!* by Roberta Grobel Intrater
Rhyme: "Señora Santa Ana / Mrs. Santa Ana"
Book: *Una sorpresa para Ana Cristina* by Margarita Robleda
Rhyme: "Lero, lero, candelero / Maker, Maker, Candlemaker"
Additional Books
Closing Activity

Program 5: Shapes / *Las formas*

Opening Activity
Motion Rhyme: "Las manitas / Little Hands"

Vocabulary Activity: "el círculo / circle"
Book: *My Very First Look at Shapes / Mi primera mirada a las formas*
  by Christiane Gunzi
Song: "Cabeza, hombros, piernas y pies / Head, shoulders, knees, and
  toes"
Additional Books
Rhyme: "Tengo manita / Here Is My Hand"
Closing Activity

Program 6: Family / *La familia*

Opening Activity
Vocabulary Activity: "la mamá or mami / mama or mommy"
Book: *Mommy! / ¡Mamá!* by Mario Ramos
Fingerplay: "Mi mamá, toda cariño, / My loving mother,"
Book: *My Grandma / Mi abuelita* by Ginger Foglesong Guy
Fingerplay: "La familia / The Family"
Book: *My Love for You / Mi amor por ti* by Susan L. Roth
Rhyme: "El reloj / The Clock"
Additional Books
Closing Activity

Program 7: Numbers / *Los números*

Opening Activity
Vocabulary Activity: "uno / one"
Book: *Numbers / Números* by Lourdes M. Alvarez
Rhyme: "Cinco pollitos / Five Baby Chicks" or "La gallina / The Hen"
Book: *Primeras palabras* by Jimena Cruz
Tickle Rhyme: "Pin-uno, pin-dos / Pen-one, Pen-two"
Book: *My Very First Look at Numbers / Mi primera mirada a los
  números* by Christiane Gunzi
Rhyme: "Calle del ocho / Eighth Street"
Additional Books
Closing Activity

Program 8: Dreams and Lullabies / *Sueños y arrullos*

Opening Activity
Book: *Goodnight Moon 1, 2, 3: A Counting Book / Buenas noches,
  luna, 1, 2, 3: Un libro para contar* by Margaret Wise Brown

Tickle Rhyme: "La luna / The Moon"
Book: *Sweet Dreams / Dulces sueños* by Pat Mora
Song: "Pimpón"
Book: *Little Night / Nochecita* by Yuyi Morales
Song: "A la rorro / Rock-a-Bye"
Rhyme: "Este niño tiene sueño / This Child Is Sleepy"
Additional Books
Closing Activity

CHAPTER 3

Program 1: ABC / 123

Opening Rhyme
Book: *Alphabet Fiesta: An English/Spanish Alphabet Story* by Anne
    Miranda
Clapping Rhyme: "El chocolate / Chocolate"
Book: *Animals from A to Z / Animales de la A a la Z* by João Coutinhas
Rhyme: "Cuéntame diez / Count to ten"
Book: *Three Friends: A Counting Book / Tres amigos: Un cuento para
    contar* by María Cristina Brusca
Call-and-Response Rhyme: "Los deditos / My Fingers"
Additional Books
Closing Rhyme: "Colorín, colorado"

Program 2: Water / *El agua*

Opening Rhyme
Book: *10 Little Rubber Ducks / 10 patitos de goma* by Eric Carle
Motion Rhyme: "Nadaban / Swimming"
Book: *¡A nadar, pececito!* by Jimena Cruz
Motion Rhyme: "Los pececitos / The Little Fish"
Book: *Hello, Ocean / Hola, mar* by Pam Muñoz Ryan
Song: "El barquito / The Little Boat"
Additional Books
Closing Rhyme

Program 3: Colors / *Los colores*

Opening Rhyme
Book: *Bright with Colors / De colores*
Rhyme: "Pito, pito, / Whistle, whistle"

Book: *Colors / Colores* by Lourdes M. Alvarez
Fingerplay: "El amarillo es mío. / Yellow is mine."
Book: *My Colors, My World / Mis colores, mi mundo* by Maya
    Christina Gonzalez
Rhyme: "A la escuela y al jardín, / At school and in the garden"
Additional Books
Closing Rhyme

Program 4: The Farm / *La granja*

Opening Rhyme
Vocabulary Activity: "la gallina / the hen"
Book: *Rooster / Gallo* by Jorge Elias Luján
Song: "Old MacDonald Had a Farm" and "La granja / The Farm"
Book: *Tomasa the Cow / La vaca Tomasa* by Christian Pietrapiana
Song: "Caballito blanco / White Pony"
Book: *Rosie's Walk / El paseo de Rosie* by Pat Hutchins
Song: "Los animalitos / The Little Animals"
Additional Books
Closing Rhyme

Program 5: Bugs / *Los insectos*

Opening Rhyme
Book: *Martina, the Beautiful Cockroach: A Cuban Folktale / Martina,*
    una cucarachita muy linda by Carmen Agra Deedy
Song: "La cucaracha / The Cockroach"
Book: *Olmo y la mariposa azul* by Alma Flor Ada or *Butterflies on*
    Carmen Street / Mariposas en la calle Carmen by Monica Brown
Movement Rhyme: "Doña Araña"
Book: *The Little Ant / La hormiga chiquita* by Michael Rose Ramirez
Motion Rhyme: "La huitsi huitsi araña / The Itsy Bitsy Spider" or "La
    hormiguita / The itsy bitsy ant"
Additional Books
Closing Rhyme

Program 6: Opposites / *Los opuestos*

Opening Rhyme
Vocabulary Activity: "*arriba*/up / *abajo*/down"
Book: *Quinito, Day and Night / Quinito, día y noche* by Ina Cumpiano
Rhyme: "Saltar / Jump"

Book: *Los opuestos* by Jimena Cruz
Vocabulary Activity: "*grande*/big / *chico*/small"
Book: *Opuestos* by Maura Gaetán
Call-and-Response Rhyme: "Los opuestos / Opposites"
Additional Books
Closing Rhyme

Program 7: The Senses / *Los sentidos*

Opening Rhyme
Vocabulary Activity: "sight / la vista"
Book: *David Smells! / ¡David huele!* by David Shannon
Call-and-Response Rhyme: "Mis cinco sentidos / My Five Senses"
Book: *¿A qué sabe? El sentido del gusto* by Maribel Suárez
Rhyme: "Una boca para comer, / One mouth to eat,"
Book: *What Can Pinky Hear? / ¿Qué puede oír Blas?* by Lucy Cousins
Motion Rhyme: "Mis manitas / My Little Hands"
Additional Books
Closing Rhyme

Program 8: Transportation / *El transporte*

Opening Rhyme
Vocabulary Activity: "el barco / boat"
Book: *How Will You Get There, Maisy? / ¿Cómo irá, Maisy?* by Lucy
   Cousins
Song: "Las ruedas del camión / The Wheels on the Bus"
Book: *How Will We Get to the Beach? / ¿Cómo iremos a la playa?* by
   Brigitte Luciani
Song: "Vamos a remar / Row Your Boat"
Book: *My Little Car / Mi carrito* by Gary Soto
Rhyme: "El que se fue a Sevilla / He Who Went to Seville"
Additional Books
Closing Rhyme

CHAPTER 4

Program 1: Animals / *Los animales*

Opening Rhyme
Vocabulary Activity: "El burro dice jijaaa, jijaaa. / The donkey says
   hee-haw, hee-haw."

Book: *Borreguita and the Coyote / Borreguita y el coyote* by Verna
   Aardema
Rhyme: "Cinco lobitos / Five Little Wolves"
Book: *The Three Pigs / Los tres cerdos: Nacho, Tito, and Miguel* by
   Bobbi Salinas
Song: "Los diez cerditos / Ten Little Pigs"
Book: *Five Little Ducks / Los cinco patitos* by Pamela Paparone
Song: "Con medio peso / With Half a Peso"
Book: *Baby Coyote and the Old Lady / El coyotito y la viejita* by
   Carmen Tafolla
Song: "Un elefante / One Elephant"
Additional Books
Closing Rhyme

Program 2: The Neighborhood / *El barrio*

Opening Rhyme
Book: *The Stranger and the Red Rooster / El forastero y el gallo rojo*
   by Victor Villaseñor
Game: "La rueda de San Miguel / The Circle of San Miguel"
Book: *Lupita's Papalote / El papalote de Lupita* by Lupe Ruiz-Flores
Game: "La comadre Juana / Comadre Juana"
Book: *Busca que te busca* by Josefina Urdaneta
Song: "La feria de San Juan / The Fair of San Juan"
Book: *We Are a Rainbow / Somos un arco iris* by Nancy Maria
   Grande Tabor
Song: "Cielito lindo"
Additional Books
Closing Rhyme

Program 3: Food / *La comida*

Opening Rhyme
Book: *Delicious Hullabaloo / Pachanga deliciosa* by Pat Mora
Song: "Plátanos y manzanas / Apples and Bananas"
Book: *The Fiesta of the Tortillas / La fiesta de las tortillas* by Jorge
   Argueta
Activity: "Tortillitas / Little Tortillas"
Book: *Too Many Tamales / Qué montón de tamales* by Gary Soto
Call-and-Response Rhyme: "Batir, batir y batir / Beat, beat, beat,"
Book: *Huevos Rancheros / Huevos rancheros* by Stefan Czernecki

Song: "Compadre, cómpreme un coco. / Compadre, buy me a coconut."
Additional Books
Closing Rhyme

Program 4: Small Creatures / *Criaturas pequeñas*

Opening Rhyme
Book: *Ramón and His Mouse / Ramón y su ratón* by Margarita Robleda
Rhyme: "Un ratoncito / A Little Mouse"
Book: *The Little Mouse / El ratoncito pequeño: A Nursery Rhyme in Spanish and English* by Pipina Salas-Porras
Rhyme: "Cinco ratoncitos / Five Little Mice"
Book: *Jump, Frog, Jump! / ¡Salta, ranita, salta!* by Robert Kalan
Rhyme: "La ranita soy yo, / I am a little frog,"
Rhyme: "Los ratones / The Mice"
Additional Books
Closing Rhyme

Program 5: Fables and Folklore / *Fábulas y folclore*

Opening Rhyme
Book: *The Lizard and the Sun / La lagartija y el sol: A Folktale in English and Spanish* by Alma Flor Ada
Song: "La planchadora / The Laundress"
Book: *The Three Javelinas / Los tres pequeños jabalíes* by Susan Lowell
Tongue Twister: "Pepe Pecas pica papas / Peter Piper picked a peck of pickled peppers."
Book: *Juan Bobo Goes to Work / Juan Bobo busca trabajo* by Marisa Montes
Rhyme: "Corre la rata. / There goes the mouse."
Additional Books
Closing Rhyme

Program 6: Family / *La familia*

Opening Rhyme
Book: *A Birthday Basket for Tía / Canasta de cumpleaños para Tía* by Pat Mora
Song: "La Tía Mónica / Aunt Monica"

Book: *What Can You Do with a Rebozo?* by Carmen Tafolla
Song: "Juanito / Little Johnny"
Book: *We Are Cousins / Somos primos* by Diane Gonzales Bertrand
Song: "Tipitín"
Additional Books
Closing Rhyme

Program 7: Festivals and Fiestas / *Los festivales y las fiestas*

Opening Rhyme
Book: *The Perfect Piñata / La piñata perfecta* by Kelli Kyle Domínguez
Song: "Bajen la piñata / Lower the Piñata" or "La piñata / The
    Piñata"
Book: *Rafi and Rosi: Carnival! / Rafi y Rosi: ¡Carnaval!* by Lulu
    Delacre
Game: "Fandango"
Book: *Birthday Swap / ¡Qué sorpresa de cumpleaños!* by Loretta
    Lopez
Song: "Las mañanitas / Mexican Birthday Song"
Additional Books
Closing Rhyme

Program 8: Letters and Words / *Las letras y palabras*

Opening Rhyme
Alphabet Sounds
Book: *Albertina Goes Up: An Alphabet Book / Albertina anda arriba:
    El abecedario* by Nancy Tabor
Song: "La mar estaba serena / The Sea Was Serene"
Book: *Mis letras favoritas* by Margarita Robleda or *Señor Felipe's
    Alphabet Adventure: El alfabeto español* by Sharon Vargo
Song: "Marcha de las letras / March of the Letters"
Additional Books
Closing Rhyme

CHAPTER 5

Program 1: Grandparents / *Los abuelos*

Opening Activity
Book: *I Love Saturdays y Domingos* by Alma Flor Ada

Song: "De colores / Colors"
Book: *Abuelita Full of Life / Abuelita, llena de vida* by Amy Costales
Song: "Arroz con leche / Rice with Milk"
Book: *In My Family / En mi familia* by Carmen Lomas Garza
Craft: *Papel Picado*
Additional Books
Closing Activity

Program 2: Birds / *Los aves*

Opening Activity
Book: *Half-Chicken / Medio pollito* by Alma Flor Ada
Craft: *Mola*
Book: *A Bicycle for Rosaura / Rosaura en bicicleta* by Daniel Barbot
Motion Rhyme: "Dos pajaritos muy sentaditos, / Two little birds"
Book: *The Bossy Gallito: A Traditional Cuban Folktale / El gallo de bodas* by Lucía M. González
Game: "Doña Blanca"
Additional Books
Closing Activity

Program 3: Soup, Tortillas, and Mexican Food / *Caldo, tortillas y comidas mexicanas*

Opening Activity
Book: *Quiquiriquí / Kikirikí* by Diane De Anda
Song: "A mi burro, a mi burro / My Donkey, My Donkey"
Book: *Magda's Tortillas / Las tortillas de Magda* by Becky Chavarría-Cháirez
Rhyme: "Tortillitas / Little Tortillas"
Book: *Mice and Beans / Arroz con frijoles y unos amables ratones* by Pam Muñoz Ryan
Song: "Hoy es lunes. / Today is Monday."
Additional Books
Closing Activity

Program 4: Ghosts, Skeletons, and the Bogeyman / *Espantos, calaveras y el cucúy*

Opening Activity
Book: *Chumba la cachumba* by Carlos Cotte

Craft: Mexican Tissue Flowers

Book: *Just a Minute: A Trickster Tale and Counting Book* by Yuyi
   Morales

Craft: *Calavera* Mask

Craft: Skeleton Puppet

Tongue Twister: "El pelo al codo / From hair to elbow"

Additional Books

Closing Activity

Program 5: Migrant Workers and the Family / *Campesinos y la familia*

Opening Activity

Book: *Tomás and the Library Lady / Tomás y la señora de la
   biblioteca* by Pat Mora

Movement Activity: "A la víbora de la mar / The Sea Serpent"

Book: *First Day in Grapes / Primer día en las uvas* by L. King Pérez

Craft: *Balero*

Additional Books

Closing Activity

Program 6: Folklore / *Folclore*

Opening Activity

Book: *Pérez and Martina / Pérez y Martina: Un cuento folklórico
   puertorriqueño* by Pura Belpré

Song: "El piojo y la pulga / The Louse and the Flea"

Book: *Doña Flor: A Tall Tale about a Giant Woman with a Great Big
   Heart / Doña Flor: Un cuento de una mujer gigante con un grande
   corazón* by Pat Mora

Game: "El florón está en la mano / The flower is in the hand"

Book: *Little Gold Star / Estrellita de oro: A Cinderella Cuento* by Joe
   Hayes

Craft: Aztec Fan

Additional Books

Closing Activity

Program 7: Famous People / *Personas famosas*

Opening Activity

Book: *The Pot That Juan Built / La vasija que Juan fabricó* by Nancy
   Andrews-Goebel

Craft: Sun Face
Book: *My Name Is Celia: The Life of Celia Cruz / Me llamo Celia: La vida de Celia Cruz* by Monica Brown
Song: "Trompo bailarín / Dancing Top"
Book: *The Storyteller's Candle / La velita de los cuentos* by Lucía González
Additional Books
Closing Activity

Program 8: Poetry / *Poesía*

Opening Activity
Book
Activity: Bilingual Poet Tree or Poetry Exchange
Rhyme: "Los diez perritos / Ten Puppies"
Closing Activity

DISCOGRAPHY OF SPANISH MUSIC FOR CHILDREN

There are many music collections on CD for children. Some of these you will have to order online via Amazon or Barnes and Noble. This is just a sampling; you may find others. The rhymes, fingerplays, and songs noted within the program section are found in one or more of these collections. If you are uncertain as to which CDs have which songs, contact your vendor. Another option is to use a search engine and type in a children's song. You are certain to find what you are looking for.

Barchas, Sarah. *Piñata! Piñata and More: Bilingual Songs for Children.* High Heaven Music, 1997.

Canciones infantiles 1. ANS, 1998.

Canciones infantiles 2. ANS, 1998.

¡Caramba! Kids. Musical Kids International, 2006.

Cri Cri. *Grandes éxitos,* Digital 2. Sony International, 1991.

———. *Juegos y juguetes.* RCA International, 1996.

———. *Playas musicales.* Sony BMG Latin, 1996.

———. *Por el mundo.* RCA International, 1996.

———. *Tiempo de aprender.* RCA International, 1996.

———. *20 éxitos.* Sony International, 2004.

———. *Verde, blanco y rojo.* Sony BMG Latin, 1996.

Hinojosa, Tish. *Every Child / Cada niño.* Rounder Records, 1996.

Las 100 clásicas de Cri Cri, Volumen 1. Sony International, 2001.

Las 100 clásicas de Cri Cri, Volumen 2. Sony International, 2001.

Líscano, Hugo, and Javier Galué. *Infantiles,* Volumen 1. Anes Records, 2000.

———. *Infantiles,* Volumen 2. Anes Records, 2000.

———. *Infantiles,* Volumen 3. Anes Records, 1998.

———. *Infantiles,* Volumen 4. Anes Records, 1999.

———. *Lo mejor de infantiles.* Anes Records, 1997.

Orozco, José-Luis. *Arrullos: Lullabies in Spanish.* Arcoiris Records, 2000.

———. *Canto y cuento.* Arcoiris Records, 2003.

———. *"De colores" and Other Latin-American Folk Songs for Children.* Arcoiris Records, 2004.

———. *Diez deditos / Ten Little Fingers and Other Play Rhymes and Action Songs from Latin America.* Arcoiris Records, 2004.

———. *Ésta es mi tierra.* Arcoiris Records, 2003.

———. *Fiestas: Celebration Songs.* Arcoiris Records, 2003.

———. *Lírica infantil con José-Luis Orozco,* Volumen 1. *Latin American Children's Folklore.* Arcoiris Records, 2000.

———. *Lírica infantil con José-Luis Orozco,* Volumen 2. *Latin American Children's Folklore.* Arcoiris Records, 2000.

———. *Lírica infantil con José-Luis Orozco,* Volumen 3. *Latin American Children's Folklore.* Arcoiris Records, 2000.

———. *Lírica infantil con José-Luis Orozco,* Volumen 4. *Animales y movimiento. Latin American Children's Folklore.* Arcoiris Records, 1995.

———. *Lírica infantil con José-Luis Orozco,* Volumen 5. *Letras, números y colores. Latin American Children's Folklore.* Arcoiris Records, 1995.

Putumayo Presents Latin Playground. Putumayo World Music, 2002.

COLLECTIONS

Each of the following books contains an assortment of nursery rhymes. Some include songs, fingerplays, games, jump-rope rhymes, and lullabies. In some of the books, musical chords are also provided. A few of them have companion CDs that can be ordered separately.

Ada, Alma Flor. *Mamá Goose: A Latino Nursery Treasury / Un tesoro de rimas infantiles.* Hyperion Books for Children, 2006.

———. *Pío Peep! Traditional Spanish Nursery Rhymes.* Illustrated by Viví Escrivá. HarperCollins, 2003.

The Baby Chicks Sing: Traditional Games, Nursery Rhymes and Songs from Spanish-Speaking Countries / Los pollitos dicen: Juegos, rimas y canciones infantiles de países de habla hispana. Little, Brown, 1994.

Castrillón, Silvia. *Tope tope tun: Tradición oral.* Editorial Norma, 1987.

Delacre, Lulu. *Arrorró, mi niño: Latino Lullabies and Gentle Games.* Lee and Low Books, 2004.

———. *Arroz con leche: Popular Songs and Rhymes from Latin America.* Scholastic, 1992.

DeSpain, Pleasant. *The Emerald Lizard: Fifteen Latin American Tales to Tell.* August House, 1999.

———. *Thirty-three Multicultural Tales to Tell.* August House, 1993.

Downs, Cynthia, and Gloria Erickson. *Hispanic Games and Rhymes: Rimas y juegos en español.* T. S. Denison, 1996.

Griego, Margot. *Tortillitas para mamá: And Other Nursery Rhymes.* Henry Holt, 1981.

Hinojosa, Tish. *Every Child / Cada niño: A Bilingual Songbook for Kids.* Cinco Puntos Press, 2002.

Longo, Alejandra. *Aserrín, aserrán: Las canciones de la abuela*. Scholastic, 2004.

Merrill, Yvonne Y. *Hands-On Latin America: Art Activities for All Ages*. KITS Publishing, 1998.

Orozco, José-Luis. *"De colores" and Other Latin-American Folk Songs for Children*. Dutton Children's Books, 1994.

———. *Diez deditos / Ten Little Fingers and Other Play Rhymes and Action Songs from Latin America*. Dutton Children's Books, 1997.

———. *Fiestas: A Year of Latin American Songs of Celebration*. Penguin Young Readers Group, 2002.

Schon, Isabel. *Tito, Tito: Rimas, adivinanzas y juegos infantiles*. Everest de Ediciones y Distribución, 1998.

Vigil, Ángel. *¡Teatro! Hispanic Plays for Young People*. Libraries Unlimited, 1996.

BIBLIOGRAPHY

Aardema, Verna. *Borreguita and the Coyote*. Knopf, 1996. Spanish:
  Borreguita y el coyote. Harcourt, 1997.
    Borreguita, a little lamb, outwits Señor Coyote.

Ada, Alma Flor. *Abecedario de los animales*. Espasa-Calpe, 1998.
    Playful animals surround and interact with the letters of the
    alphabet.

———. *Gathering the Sun: An Alphabet in Spanish and English*. Lothrop,
  1997.
    This book of poetry shows workers in the field and the fruits of
    their labor.

———. *Half-Chicken / Medio pollito*. Illustrated by Kim Howard.
  Doubleday, 1997.
    Why do weather vanes have roosters on the top? This traditional
    folktale explains why and introduces us to Half-Chicken. He has
    one eye, one leg, and one wing!

———. *La hamaca de la vaca, o, Un amigo mas*. Santillana USA, 2000.
    This is a short collection of simple stories and rhymes.

———. *I Love Saturdays y Domingos*. Illustrated by Elivia Savadier.
  Atheneum Books for Young Readers, 2002.
    A young girl of dual heritage splits her weekends between English-
    and Spanish-speaking grandparents. Despite the differences
    in language and culture, she understands that the love of her
    grandparents has no boundaries.

————. *The Lizard and the Sun / La lagartija y el sol: A Folktale in English and Spanish*. Bantam Books, 1997.
> When the sun disappears from the sky, a lizard's persistence pays off when he finds the sun and becomes a hero.

————. *Olmo y la mariposa azul*. Laredo Publishing, 1992.
> A young boy named Olmo wakes up one morning to find a butterfly in his room, which he immediately follows as it flies out his window.

————. *The Rooster Who Went to His Uncle's Wedding: A Latin American Folktale*. Putnam, 1993. Spanish: *El gallo que fue a la boda de su tío: Cuento popular hispanoamericano*. Putnam and Grosset Group, 1998.
> In this cumulative folktale from Latin America, the sun sets off a chain of events that results in the cleaning of Rooster's beak in time for his uncle's wedding.

Aigner-Clark, Julie. *Asómate y ve los números*. Advanced Marketing, 2003.
> This is a Baby Einstein book with an adventure with numbers.

Alarcón, Francisco X. *Angels Ride Bikes and Other Fall Poems / Los ángeles andan en bicicleta y otros poemas de otoño*. Illustrated by Maya Christina Gonzalez. Children's Book Press, 1999.
> This title is the latest addition to Alarcón's award-winning anthologies of poems representing recollections of the author's childhood spent in Mexico and Los Angeles.

————. *Animal Poems of the Iguazú / Animalario del Iguazú*. Children's Book Press, 2008.
————. *From the Bellybutton of the Moon: And Other Summer Poems / Del ombligo de la luna: Y otros poemas de verano*. Children's Book Press, 2005.
————. *Iguanas in the Snow: And Other Winter Poems / Iguanas en la nieve: Y otros poemas de invierno*. Children's Book Press, 2005.
————. *Laughing Tomatoes and Other Spring Poems / Jitomates risueños y otros poemas de primavera*. Illustrated by Maya Christina González. Children's Book Press, 1997.
> The Mexican American poet Alarcón presents a bilingual collection of poems about family, nature, and tradition based on songs that his grandmother taught him.

Alcántara, Ricardo. *¡Caramba con los amigos!* Combel, 2000.
> Florián and friends are playing quite well until it comes to sharing food.

All about Baby / Todo sobre bebé. DK Publishing, 2004.
    This simple board book shows baby's world in photographs.

Altman, Linda Jacobs. *Amelia's Road*. Lee and Low Books, 1993. Spanish:
    El camino de Amelia. Lee and Low Books, 1993.
    Amelia longs to have a place that she and her migrant worker
    family can call home.

Alvarez, Lourdes M. *Alphabet*. Sweetwater Press, 2005. Spanish: *Alfabeto*.
    Sweetwater Press, 2005.
———. *Colors*. Sweetwater Press, 2004. Spanish: *Colores*. Sweetwater
    Press, 2004.
———. *Numbers*. Sweetwater Press, 2005. Spanish: *Números*. Sweetwater
    Press, 2005.
———. *Shapes*. Sweetwater Press, 2005. Spanish: *Formas*. Sweetwater
    Press, 2005.
    Each of these books by Lourdes Alvarez is part of a series of
    board books called My First Book. They are available in separate
    Spanish and English editions and contain bright, colorful
    illustrations.

Amado, Elisa. *Cousins*. Groundwood Books, 2004. Spanish: *Primas*.
    Libros Tigrillos, 2003.
    Two cousins, each living with a different grandmother, visit each other.

Ancona, George. *Barrio: José's Neighborhood*. Harcourt Brace, 1998.
    Spanish: *Barrio: El barrio de José*. Harcourt Brace, 1998.
    Ancona presents photographs of a young boy's neighborhood in
    San Francisco.

———. *My House / Mi casa*. Children's Press, 2004.
    Araceli and her family move to the United States from Mexico in
    this bilingual book.

———. *My Neighborhood / Mi barrio*. Children's Press, 2004.
    This bilingual book features a child's neighborhood in Brooklyn.

Andrews-Goebel, Nancy. *The Pot That Juan Built*. Illustrated by David
    Diaz. Lee and Low Books, 2002. Spanish: *La vasija que Juan fabricó*.
    Lee and Low Books, 2004.
    The life of Juan Quezada is radiantly depicted, and the text
    follows the rhyme of "The House That Jack Built."

Anzaldúa, Gloria. *Prietita and the Ghost Woman / Prietita y La Llorona.* Children's Book Press, 1996.
> Prietita, a young Mexican American girl, becomes lost in her search for the herb to cure her mother and is aided by a legendary ghost woman.

Argueta, Jorge. *Alfredito Flies Home.* Groundwood Books, 2008. Spanish: *Alfredito regresa volando a su casa.* Groundwood Books, 2007.
> Alfredito and his family are getting ready for their airplane trip to their old home in El Salvador.

———. *The Fiesta of the Tortillas / La fiesta de las tortillas.* Alfaguara, 2006.
> Argueta recounts a mystery from his childhood involving tortillas at his family's restaurant in El Salvador.

Ashbé, Jeanne. *¡Eso no se hace!* Editorial Corimbo, 2001.
> This book shows how a baby shouldn't behave.

Avalos, Cecilia. *La fiesta del abecedario.* Sundance, 1993.
> This is a poem about a Mexican fiesta featuring the letters of the alphabet.

Baca, Ana. *Benito's Sopaipillas / Las sopaipillas de Benito.* Piñata Books, 2006.
> As they prepare to make the traditional pastry called a *sopaipilla,* Christina's grandmother tells her a story about the first *sopaipilla.*

———. *Chiles for Benito / Chiles para Benito.* Piñata Books, 2003.
> Christina's grandmother tells her the story of how her great-grandfather was given the magical chile seeds to make the chile pepper.

Baker, Alan. *Little Rabbits' First Number Book.* Kingfisher, 1998. Spanish: *Los números.* Kingfisher, 2003.
> This is a very simple book about numbers.

Banks, Kate. *Fox.* Farrar, Straus, and Giroux, 2007. Spanish: *El zorrito.* Editorial Juventud, 2007.
> A baby fox anticipates the time when he can go out alone, but first his parents must teach him the way of the wilderness.

Barbot, Daniel. *A Bicycle for Rosaura.* Illustrated by Morella Fuenmayor. Kane/Miller, 1994. Spanish: *Rosaura en bicicleta.* Sagebrush Education Resources, 1992.
> A hen named Rosaura wants a bicycle for her birthday. Find out what happens when she gets one!

Beaton, Clare. *Colors / Los colores.* Barron's, 1997.
    Learn colors with teddy bears.

———. *Family / La familia.* Barron's, 1997.
    Teddy bears introduce you to family.

Belpré, Pura. *Pérez and Martina.* Warne, 1960. Spanish: *Pérez y Martina: Un cuento folklórico puertorriqueño.* Warne, 1966.
    This is a retelling of a traditional tale about the romance between Pérez the mouse and Martina the cockroach.

Benatar, Raquel. *Isabel Allende: Memories for a Story / Isabel Allende: Recuerdos para un cuento.* Piñata Books, 2004.
    Here is the story of young Isabel, who found comfort among old books in the basement of her grandparents' home in Chile.

Bernardo, Anilú. *A Day with My Aunts / Un día con mis tías.* Piñata Books, 2006.
    A young girl talks about her special day spent with her aunts.

Bernier-Grand, Carmen T. *César: ¡Sí, se puede! Yes, We Can!* Illustrated by David Diaz. Marshall Cavendish, 2004.
    Bernier-Grand's poems flawlessly intertwine Spanish words into the English text, which includes prayers, folk sayings, and César Chávez's own words.

Bertrand, Diane Gonzales. *Sip, Slurp, Soup, Soup / Caldo, caldo, caldo.* Piñata Books, 1997.
    A rhythmic text with repetitive phrases relates how the children watch Mamá make soup and then go with Papá to get tortillas before enjoying the *caldo.*

———. *We Are Cousins / Somos primos.* Piñata Books, 2007.
    Family is the theme of this bilingual book. It explores many things that cousins share—like grandparents, which means sharing laps and hugs as well.

Blackstone, Stella. *Bear on a Bike.* Barefoot Books, 2001. Spanish: *Oso en bicicleta.* Barefoot Books, 2003.
    Bear goes for a ride on his bike in this book that is part of the Bear series.

Blanco, Alberto. *ABC.* Sistemas Técnicos de Edición, 2001.
    Each letter of the alphabet is shown with a word that starts with that letter.

Boynton, Sandra. *Moo, Baa, La La La*. Simon and Schuster, 1984. Spanish: *Muu, beee. ¡Así fue!* Simon and Schuster Libros para Niños, 2003.
> Have fun making animal sounds in this simple board book for very young children.

Bright with Colors / De colores. Marshall Cavendish, 2008.
> The Caldecott medalist David Diaz illustrated this book, which has words to the traditional song "De colores."

Brown, Margaret Wise. *Big Red Barn*. HarperCollins, 1994. Spanish: *El gran granero rojo*. HarperCollins, 1996.
> Visit the farm and see the animals that live there.

———. *Goodnight Moon 1, 2, 3: A Counting Book / Buenas noches, luna, 1, 2, 3: Un libro para contar*. Rayo, 2007.
> Here is a bilingual offering in board-book format featuring familiar images from *Goodnight Moon*.

Brown, Monica. *Butterflies on Carmen Street / Mariposas en la calle Carmen*. Arte Público Press, 2007.
> Julianita is excited because today she will receive her very own caterpillar to raise.

———. *My Name Is Celia: The Life of Celia Cruz / Me Llamo Celia: La Vida de Celia Cruz*. Luna Rising, 2004.
> The life of Celia Cruz is engagingly depicted.

———. *My Name Is Gabito: The Life of Gabriel García Márquez / Me llamo Gabito: La vida de Gabriel García Márquez*. Luna Rising, 2007.
> Gabito was born in Colombia, and his imagination takes him to faraway places. He grows up to be an important writer.

Brusca, María Cristina. *The Blacksmith and the Devils*. Henry Holt, 1992. Spanish: *El herrero y el diablo*. Henry Holt, 1992.
> Juan Pobreza makes a deal with the devil.

———. *Three Friends: A Counting Book / Tres amigos: Un cuento para contar*. Henry Holt, 1995.
> Meet cows, horses, tumbleweeds, coyotes, snakes, cacti, and two hapless cowpokes who try to lasso them all in this rollicking southwestern adventure that counts up to ten and down again.

Busquets, Jordi. *Hoy vamos de viaje*. Susaeta, 2005.
> In this illustrated board book for children, the little animals use different types of transportation.

———. *Mis amigos de la granja.* Susaeta, 2005.
  This illustrated board book for children presents the names of
  some of the domestic animals of the farm.

Carle, Eric. *Colors / Colores.* Penguin Young Readers Group, 2008.
  This board book features colors for very young children.

———. *10 Little Rubber Ducks.* HarperCollins, 2005. Spanish: *10 patitos
  de goma.* Rayo, 2007.
  Ten rubber ducks are swept off a cargo ship during a storm.

———. *The Very Busy Spider.* Philomel Books, 1984. Spanish: *La araña
  muy ocupada.* Philomel Books, 2008.
  Here is a lap-sized version of Carle's book about a spider that sets
  out to spin her web.

———. *The Very Hungry Caterpillar.* Philomel Books, 1987. Spanish: *La
  oruga muy hambrienta.* Philomel Books, 1989.
  A very hungry caterpillar proceeds to eat her way through
  different foods.

Carrier, Isabelle. *¿Un pequeño qué?* Edelvives, 2003.
  An elephant child tries to figure out what his parents mean when
  they say they are waiting for a baby elephant.

Carril, Isabel. *Descubro las formas.* Bruño, 2007.
  This is a lift-the-flap board book about shapes.

Castañeda, Omar S. *Abuela's Weave.* Illustrated by Enrique O. Sánchez.
  Lee and Low Books, 1995. Spanish: *El tapiz de abuela.* Lee and Low
  Books, 1993.
  Surrounded by the colorful terrain of the Guatemalan countryside,
  a young girl learns the traditional art of weaving from her
  grandmother.

Ceelen, Vicky. *Baby! Baby!* Random House, 2008.
  This wordless book shows babies facing an animal in a similar
  pose or with a similar look.

Chavarría-Cháirez, Becky. *Magda's Tortillas / Las tortillas de Magda.*
  Piñata Books, 2000.
  While learning to make tortillas on her seventh birthday, Magda
  tries to make perfectly round ones like those her grandmother
  makes, but instead she creates a variety of wonderful shapes.

Cisneros, Sandra. *Hairs / Pelitos.* Knopf, 1997.
>A young girl describes how everyone in her family has different types of hair.

Corpi, Lucha. *Where Fireflies Dance / Ahí, donde bailan las luciérnagas.* Illustrated by Mira Reisberg. Children's Book Press, 1997.
>Lucha and her brother Victor love to hear their grandmother's story of San Sebastián, a ghost said to haunt a local house.

Costales, Amy. *Abuelita Full of Life / Abuelita, llena de vida.* Luna Rising, 2007.
>José's grandmother moves from Mexico to his house.

Cotte, Carlos. *Chumba la cachumba.* Ediciones Ekaré, 1995.
>Every hour, on the hour, the skeletons come out to play, sing, and have fun, all the while chanting, "Chumba la cachumba, la cachumbabá."

Cousins, Lucy. *How Will You Get There, Maisy?* Candlewick Press, 2004. Spanish: *¿Cómo irá, Maisy?* Serres, 2004.
>Follow Maisy and her friends as they use a variety of vehicles to get to where they are going.

———. *What Can Pinky Hear?* Candlewick Press, 1997. Spanish: *¿Qué puede oír Blas?* Serres, 1997.
>Pinky hears noises in the sky and in the trees.

Coutinhas, João. *Animals from A to Z / Animales de la A a la Z.* Everest, 2003.
>A bilingual text that introduces the alphabet to preschoolers with animal names.

Cruz, Jimena. *¡A nadar, pececito!* Editorial Sigmar, 2007.
>Little fish swim away from the dangers in the ocean.

———. *Animales del mar.* Editorial Sigmar, 2007.
>Here is a book showing many animals of the sea.

———. *Los colores.* Editorial Sigmar, 2007.
>This is an illustrated board book for children with images and textures for seeing, touching, and learning colors and other words.

———. *Los opuestos.* Editorial Sigmar, 2007.
>This book is part of a series called Colección sonrisas. This one is a board book about opposites with textures to feel.

———. *Primeras palabras*. Editorial Sigmar, 2007.
> This is a board book about first words, also part of a series called Colección sonrisas.

Cumpiano, Ina. *Quinito, Day and Night / Quinito, dia y noche*. Children's Book Press, 2008.
> This is a book about opposites, and Quinito is a young child.

Czernecki, Stefan. *Huevos Rancheros*. Crocodile Books, 2001. Spanish: *Huevos rancheros*. Artes de México el Mundo, 2002.
> Marcelina is a hen that escapes to the country and lays eggs for Padre Tomás.

De Anda, Diane. *Quiquiriquí / Kikirikí*. Piñata Books, 2004.
> Marta and Celia are horrified to learn that their family plans to eat the rooster their *abuela* brought home, and they set out to save him.

Deedy, Carmen Agra. *Martina, the Beautiful Cockroach: A Cuban Folktale*. Peachtree, 2007. Spanish: *Martina, una cucarachita muy linda*. Peachtree, 2007.
> This is based on the folktale of Martina, a too-particular cockroach and her suitors.

Delacre, Lulu. *Nathan's Balloon Adventure*. Scholastic, 1991.
> An elephant named Nathan takes a trip in a hot-air balloon.

———. *Rafi and Rosi: Carnival!* Rayo, 2008. Spanish: *Rafi y Rosi: ¡Carnaval!* Rayo, 2006.
> Rafi and Rosi enjoy the festival of carnival.

Denou, Violeta. *Teo descubre los medios de transporte*. Grupo Editorial Ceac, 1998.
> Teo finds out about all kinds of transportation.

———. *Teo en avión*. Planeta Publishing, 2004.
> A child named Teo flies an airplane.

———. *Teo encuentra los errores: Un paseo en barco*. Grupo Editorial Ceac, 2000.
> Teo takes a boat trip.

———. *Teo se va de viaje*. Planeta Publishing, 2004.
> Teo goes for a ride.

Díaz-Toledo, Alonso. *¡A desayunar!* Susaeta, 2005.
> This is a board book with questions about what to eat for breakfast.

———. *¡A dormir!* Susaeta, 2005.
> A child asks about things he uses at bedtime in this board book for very young children.

Dodd, Emma. *123 Lolo: Un cuento sobre números y colores.* Random House, 2004.
> Learn numbers and colors with Lolo, the dog in this board book.

Domínguez, Kelli Kyle. *The Perfect Piñata / La piñata perfecta.* Albert Whitman, 2002.
> Marisa picks out the most beautiful piñata and then decides she can't possibly break it at her birthday party.

Dorros, Arthur. *Abuela.* Dutton, 1991. Spanish: *Abuela.* Dutton, 1995.
> A child and her grandmother take an imaginary flight over their city.

———. *Radio Man / Don Radio.* Harper, 1993.
> Diego relies on the radio to stay connected as his migrant family travels for seasonal work.

Dupuis, Sylvia. *Las diez gallinas.* Edelvives/Editorial Luis Vives, 2006.
> Ten hens each lay an egg in a different place in this board book for young children.

Ehlert, Lois. *Cuckoo: A Mexican Folktale / Cucu: Un cuento folklórico mexicano.* Translated by Gloria de Aragón Andujar. Harcourt, 1997.
> The birds agree at the end of this brightly colored picture book that "you can't tell much about a bird by looking at its feathers."

———. *Moon Rope: A Peruvian Folktale / Un lazo a la luna: Una leyenda peruana.* Harcourt Brace Jovanovich, 1992.
> Fox and Mole try to climb to the moon in this Peruvian folktale.

Elya, Susan Middleton. *Bebé Goes Shopping.* Harcourt, 2006.
> Bebé goes shopping with his mother in this book that has some Spanish words.

Emberly, Rebecca. *My Opposites / Mis opuestos.* Little, Brown, 2000.
> Bright, colorful pictures in this board book for babies and toddlers will be useful in teaching the concept of opposites.

———. *My Shapes / Mis formas.* Little, Brown, 2000.
> This board book is part of a series of board books that introduce concepts for very young children.

Espinoza, Gerald. *Los pollitos dicen.* Ediciones Ekaré, 2007.
>   Mamá and her baby chicks live in a house in this board book that
>   follows the words of the song by the same name.

Facklam, Margery. *Bugs for Lunch / Insectos para el almuerzo.*
> Charlesbridge, 2002.
>   Different bug-eating animals are shown throughout this book.

Fernández, Laura. *¿Qué veo? El sentido de la vista.* Grijalbo, 1995.
>   A little bird points out all he sees.

Figuerola, Mercedes. *Los contrarios.* Susaeta, 2005.
>   This board book uses lift-the-flap features to introduce opposites.

Foster, Karen Sharp. *Good Night, My Little Chicks / Buenas noches, mis*
> *pollitos.* Illustrated by Maritza Davila McKee. First Story Press, 1997.
>   The story of young Carlos's preparations for bed is intertwined
>   with the Latin American folksong "Los pollitos."

Franco, Betsy. *Vamos a la granja de la abuela.* Children's Press, 2003.
>   While traveling to visit Grandma on her farm, a family from the
>   city uses various modes of transportation.

Gaetán, Maura. *Colors / Colores.* Editorial Sigmar, 2006.
>   This board book with movable parts has animals asking questions
>   about colors.

———. *Un día en colores: Un libro sobre colores.* Editorial Sigmar, 2006.
>   A child goes to the beach with his toys in this board book.

———. *Opuestos.* Editorial Sigmar, 2006.
>   Young children will learn about some opposites in this board book
>   with movable parts.

———. *¿Qué forma tiene? Un libro sobre formas.* Editorial Sigmar, 2006.
>   Another book in this series of board books is a simple look at
>   shapes.

Galindo, Claudia. *Do You Know the Cucuy? / ¿Conoces al cucuy?* Piñata
> Books, 2008.
>   A child meets the *Cucuy*, who turns out not to be the scary
>   creature her *papá* has warned her about.

Gomi, Taro. *My Friends / Mis amigos.* Chronicle Books, 2006.
>   A child learns to walk with help from her mostly animal friends.

González, Ada Acosta. *Mayte and the Bogeyman / Mayte y el cuco*. Piñata Books, 2006.
> Mayte and Pepito follow the ice cream seller, who they are sure is the bogeyman.

González, Lucía. *The Bossy Gallito: A Traditional Cuban Folktale / El gallo de bodas*. Scholastic, 1994.
> On the way to the wedding of his Tío Períco, a bossy little rooster spies two kernels of corn just waiting to be eaten.

———. *The Storyteller's Candle / La velita de los cuentos*. Children's Book Press, 2008.
> A glimpse into Pura Belpré's work as a children's librarian is told in this story.

González, Marifé. *Aprende las letras*. Susaeta, 2004.
> In this illustrated book for children, a little dog presents letters inside words from his daily activities.

Gonzales, Maya Christina. *My Colors, My World / Mis colores, mi mundo*. Children's Book Press, 2007.
> The author explores the colors of the desert in this bilingual book, which received a 2008 Pura Belpré honor award for illustration.

Grez, M. *Contamos 10 en el mar*. Susaeta, 2005.
> In this board book for children, the readers can count from one to ten and get to know by name ten sea creatures.

Griswold del Castillo, Richard. *César Chávez: The Struggle for Justice / César Chávez: La lucha por la justicia*. Piñata Books, 2008.
> The life of César Chávez is told in this bilingual book.

Gunzi, Christiane. *My Very First Look at Colors*. Two-Can Publishing, 1997. Spanish: *Mi primera mirada a los colores*. Two-Can Publishing, 2004.
> Photographs explore the concept of color, from red strawberries and a yellow duck to blue marbles and other colorful objects.

———. *My Very First Look at Numbers*. Two-Can Publishing, 2006. Spanish: *Mi primera mirada a los números*. Two-Can Publishing, 2004.
> This simple book filled with colorful photographs introduces numbers.

———. *My Very First Look at Shapes*. Two-Can Publishing, 2006. Spanish: *Mi primera mirada a las formas*. Two-Can Publishing, 2004.
> This simple book introduces shapes.

Guy, Ginger Foglesong. *My Grandma / Mi abuelita*. HarperCollins, 2007.
 A young boy visits his grandmother in the country in this bilingual
 book.

Hayes, Joe. *The Day It Snowed Tortillas: Tales from Spanish New Mexico*.
 Cinco Puntos Press, 2003.
 This is a collection of folklore from New Mexico.

————. *Little Gold Star / Estrellita de oro: A Cinderella Cuento*.
 Illustrated by Gloria Osuna Pérez and Lucía Angela Pérez. Cinco
 Puntos Press, 2000.
 This book offers a special interpretation of Cinderella that is
 popular in the mountain communities of New Mexico.

Herrera, Juan Felipe. *Calling the Doves / El canto de las palomas*.
 Children's Book Press, 1995.
 Herrera brings to life the everyday experiences of his childhood
 among migrant workers.

————. *Grandma and Me at the Flea / Los meros meros remateros*.
 Children's Book Press, 2002.
 Juanito accompanies his grandmother to a flea market in southern
 California, where he helps her and the other vendors.

————. *The Upside-Down Boy / El niño de cabeza*. Children's Book Press,
 2000.
 Herrera tells about the year that he was able to attend school for
 the very first time.

Hutchins, Pat. *Rosie's Walk*. Simon and Schuster Children's Publishing,
 1968. Spanish: *El paseo de Rosie*. Simon and Schuster Children's
 Publishing, 1997.
 Rosie the hen takes a leisurely walk, unaware of possible danger.

Inaraja, Javier. *El conejito volador*. Susaeta, 2005.
 In this board book, a little rabbit decides he wants to fly like a bird.

————. *La granja*. Susaeta, 2005.
 This board book has a touch-and-feel feature and shows farm animals.

Intrater, Roberta Grobel. *Eat!* Scholastic, 2002. Spanish: *¡Que rico!*
 Scholastic, 2002.
 This board book features photographs of babies learning to eat.

————. *Hugs and Kisses*. Scholastic, 2002. Spanish: *Besitos y abrazos*.
 Scholastic, 2002.
 This board book shows pictures of parents hugging and kissing
 their babies.

————. *Sleepyheads*. Scholastic, 2002. *Dulces sueños*. Scholastic, 2002.
Photographs of sleepy babies fill the pages of this book.

————. *Splish, Splash*. Scholastic, 2002. Spanish: *¡Al agua, patos!*
Scholastic, 2002.
This book contains photographs of babies enjoying water.

Jiménez, Francisco. *La mariposa*. Houghton Mifflin, 1998.
Because he can speak only Spanish, Francisco has trouble when
he begins first grade, but his fascination with the caterpillar in the
classroom helps him begin to fit in.

Kalan, Robert. *Jump, Frog, Jump!* Greenwillow Books, 1981. Spanish:
¡Salta, ranita, salta! Greenwillow Books, 1994.
Watch out, Frog, and keep jumping out of harm's way.

Katz, Karen. *Where Is Baby's Belly Button?* Simon and Schuster Children's
Publishing, 2000. Spanish: *¿Dónde está el ombliguito?* Simon and
Schuster Libros para Niños, 2004.
Lift the tabs to find baby's eyes, nose, and belly button!

Kleven, Elisa. *Hooray, a Piñata!* Penguin, 2000. Spanish: *¡Viva! ¡Una
piñata!* Penguin Young Readers Group, 1996.
Clara loves her piñata, which is made to look like a dog, and she
pretends it is really her pet.

Krull, Kathleen. *Harvesting Hope: The Story of César Chávez*. Illustrated
by Yuyi Morales. Harcourt, 2003. Spanish: *Cosechando esperanza: La
historia de César Chávez*. Harcourt, 2003.
The life of César Chávez is beautifully portrayed and tells of
young César and his work that led to the establishment of the
United Farm Workers Association.

Levy, Janice. *Celebrate! It's Cinco de Mayo! / ¡Celebremos! ¡Es el cinco de
mayo!* Albert Whitman, 2007.
A young boy celebrates with his family at this event that is a
celebration of the Mexican army's victory over France in 1862.
Activities are included.

Lomas Garza, Carmen. *In My Family / En mi familia*. Children's Book
Press, 1996.
The author describes, in bilingual text and illustrations, her
experiences growing up in a Hispanic community in Texas.

Lopez, Loretta. *Birthday Swap*. Lee and Low Books, 1997. Spanish: *¡Qué sorpresa de cumpleaños!* Lee and Low Books, 1997.
> Two sisters swap birthdays so that the younger one can celebrate hers in the summer.

López de Mariscal, Blanca. *The Harvest Birds / Los pájaros de la cosecha*. Illustrated by Enrique Flores. Children's Book Press, 1995.
> Set in southern Mexico, this folktale features the farmer Juan Zanate, who listens to the advice of birds and replants the weeds around the outside of his field.

Lowell, Susan. *The Three Javelinas / Los tres pequeños jabalíes*. Illustrated by Jim Harris. Northland, 1996.
> This southwestern adaptation of "The Three Little Pigs" features the bristly haired javelina.

Luciani, Brigitte. *How Will We Get to the Beach? / ¿Cómo iremos a la playa?* North-South Books, 2003.
> The reader is asked to guess what Roxanne must leave behind as she tries various means of transportation to get to the beach.

Luenn, Nancy. *A Gift for Abuelita: Celebrating the Day of the Dead / Un regalo para abuelita: En celebración del día de los muertos*. Illustrated by Robert Chapman. Rising Moon, 1998.
> When her *abuelita* dies, Rosita's grandfather tells her that she can make a gift for the Day of the Dead, a memorial day, celebrated in many Mexican American communities.

Luján, Jorge Elias. *Rooster / Gallo*. Groundwood Books, 2004.
> This simple book shows a rooster and how he wakes up with the sun.

Madrigal, Antonio Hernández. *Blanca's Feather / La pluma de Blanca*. Rising Moon, 2001.
> Rosalía searches for her hen, Blanca, for the annual blessing of the animals.

Mantoni, Elisa. *At School / En el colegio*. Everest, 2005.
> Animals show different items at school.

Marcuse, Aída E. *A Piece of Bread / Un trozo de pan*. Panamericana Editorial, 2005.
> What happens when rabbit steals duck's bread?

Martín Gimeno, Lourdes. *Conoce los colores.* Susaeta, 2005.
> In this illustrated board book for children, a little bear presents things in basic colors.

Marzollo, Jean. *I Am Water.* Scholastic, 1996. Spanish: *Soy el agua.* Scholastic, 1999.
> Find out many of the purposes that water serves.

McDonald, Jill. *The Itsy Bitsy Spider.* Scholastic, 2007. Spanish: *La araña chiquitita.* Scholastic, 2007.
> The ever-persistent spider climbs up the waterspout in this board book.

Miranda, Anne. *Alphabet Fiesta: An English/Spanish Alphabet Story.* Turtle Books, 2001.
> All of Zelda's friends from A to Z make their way to the zoo to surprise her on her birthday.

Montes, Marisa. *Juan Bobo Goes to Work.* HarperCollins, 2000. Spanish: *Juan Bobo busca trabajo.* HarperCollins, 2006.
> Poor, silly Juan Bobo just can't seem to get things right.

Mora, Pat. *Agua, agua, agua.* Scott, Foresman, 1995.
> A retelling of Aesop's fable of the crow that was able to obtain a drink of water by dropping pebbles one by one into the source of the water.

———. *The Bakery Lady / La señora de la panadería.* Piñata Books, 2001.
> Monica, who wants to be a baker like her grandmother, finds the doll hidden in the bread on the feast of the Three Kings and thus gets to bake cookies for the next fiesta.

———. *A Birthday Basket for Tía.* Maxwell Macmillan International, 1992. Spanish: *Canasta de cumpleaños para Tía.* Lectorum Publications, 1992.
> With help and interference from her cat, Chica, Cecilia prepares a surprise gift for her great-aunt's ninetieth birthday.

———. *Confetti: Poems for Children.* Illustrated by Enrique O. Sánchez. Lee and Low Books, 1999.
> Joyful, rhythmic poems—all with Mexican American or southwestern themes—elicit movement, color, and dance.

———. *Delicious Hullabaloo / Pachanga deliciosa.* Piñata Books, 1998.
> It is time for the animals to gather and share in the festivities that a late-night snack brings, along with the music of the mariachi band, in this poetic journey.

———. *The Desert Is My Mother / El desierto es mi madre*. Piñata Books, 1994.
> A poetic depiction of the desert as the provider of comfort, food, spirit, and life.

———. *Doña Flor: A Tall Tale about a Giant Woman with a Great Big Heart*. Illustrated by Raul Colón. Knopf, 2005. Spanish: *Doña Flor: Un cuento de una mujer gigante con un grande corazón*. Dragonfly Books, 2005.
> Mora's poetic language brings to life this original and engaging character whose love and concern for her neighbors and friends fills the story with joy.

———. *Here, Kitty, Kitty! / ¡Ven, gatita, ven!* Rayo, 2008.
> Kitty hides each time he is called. This book is part of a series published by Rayo, an imprint of HarperCollins.

———. *Let's Eat! / ¡A comer!* Rayo, 2008.
> A family enjoys a meal together.

———. *¡Marimba! Animales from A to Z*. Clarion Books, 2006.
> When the zookeepers fall asleep, the animals are ready to sing and dance!

———. *Sweet Dreams / Dulces sueños*. Rayo, 2008.
> It is time for bed, so close your eyes and have sweet dreams.

———. *Tomás and the Library Lady*. Random House, 1997. Spanish: *Tomás y la señora de la biblioteca*. Dragonfly Books, 1997.
> While helping his family in their work as migrant laborers far from their home, Tomás finds an entire world to explore in the books at the local public library.

———. *Uno, Dos, Tres: 1, 2, 3*. Clarion, 1996.
> Two sisters go shopping for a birthday present for their mother.

Morales, Yuyi. *Just a Minute: A Trickster Tale and Counting Book*. Chronicle Books, 2003.
> When Señor Calavera, or Death, comes to take Grandma Beetle as her time has come, she answers with "just a minute."

———. *Little Night*. Roaring Brook Press, 2007. Spanish: *Nochecita*. Roaring Brook Press, 2007.
> It is time for Little Night to go to bed, so Mother Sky is there to help her.

Moretón, Daniel. *La Cucaracha Martina: A Caribbean Folktale*. Turtle
Books, 1997. Spanish: *La cucaracha Martina: Un cuento folklórico del
Caribe*. Turtle Books, 1997.
A too-particular cockroach dismisses one suitor after another.

Nava, Emanuela. *Arrullos y caricias*. Anaya, 2006.
In this board book, Peter Rabbit spends day and night playing.

———. *Una comida sorpresa*. Anaya, 2006.
In this board book, Peter Rabbit and his friends discover fun ways
to play with their food before eating it.

———. *Gotas y goterones*. Anaya, 2006.
In this board book, Peter Rabbit and friends get dirty after a
storm comes in.

———. *Una merienda de hielo*. Anaya, 2006.
In this board book, Peter Rabbit plays in the snow with his friends.

Nazoa, Aquiles. *Fábula de la ratoncita presumida*. Ediciones Ekaré–Banco
del Libro, 1990.
After much searching for a husband, a proud mouse happily
accepts the same mouse she had previously rejected.

Nodar, Carmen Santiago. *Abuelita's Paradise*. A. Whitman, 1992. Spanish:
El paraíso de abuelita. A. Whitman, 1992.
Marita has fond memories of her grandma.

Nye, Naomi Shihab. *The Tree Is Older Than You Are: A Bilingual
Gathering of Poems and Stories from Mexico with Paintings by
Mexican Artists*. Simon and Schuster, 1995.
Various regions in Mexico are represented in this exquisite
anthology, which includes selections written in Spanish as well as
in two Mayan languages.

Palomar de Miguel, Juan. *Mis primeras letras de palabras mexicanas*.
Ediciones Destino, 2004.
This illustrated Spanish-language alphabet book for children uses
Mexican vocabulary.

Paparone, Pamela. *Five Little Ducks*. North-South Books, 2005. Spanish:
Los cinco patitos. North-South Books, 2007.
Five little ducks get lost, one by one, so Mamá goes out to find them.

Peek, Merle. *Roll Over! A Counting Song / ¡Dénse vuelta! Una canción de
cuentos*. Clarion Books, 2008.

Written to the words of the song, this board book has a child's stuffed animals rolling off the bed, one by one.

Perea Estrada, Altamira. *Un abecedario muy sabroso*. Scholastic, 1996.
Animals introduce the alphabet to readers in this simple ABC book.

Pérez, Amada Irma. *Nana's Big Surprise / ¡Nana, qué sorpresa!* Children's Book Press, 2007.
Amada and her family build a chicken coop for Grandma, who is grieving the death of Grandpa.

Pérez, L. King. *First Day in Grapes*. Lee and Low Books, 2002. Spanish: *Primer día en las uvas*. Lee and Low Books, 2004.
Chico's first day of school is correlated with the crop his migrant family will be harvesting.

Pietrapiana, Christian. *Tomasa the Cow / La vaca Tomasa*. Arte Público Press, 1999.
Tomasa the cow leaves the farm in her quest for freedom.

Prims, Marta. *I Am a Little Spider / Soy una pequeña araña*. Barron's, 2002.
A little spider recounts her life in this board book for children.

Put, Klaartje van der. *El ratón Pimpón*. Bruño, 2006.
A mouse named Pimpón lives in an upside-down flowerpot in this board book with puppet insert.

Ramirez, Michael Rose. *The Little Ant / La hormiga chiquita*. Rizzoli, 1995.
A little ant seeks restitution from the humans, animals, and natural events it holds responsible for its broken leg.

Ramos, Mario. *Mommy! / ¡Mamá!* Corimbo, 2007.
A child goes from room to room looking for Mommy.

Ranchetti, Sebastiano. *Animal Opposites / Opuestos animales*. Gareth Stevens Publishing, 2008.
Animals introduce opposites for young children.

Rigol, Francesc. *Animales de la granja*. Susaeta, 2005.
See the animals on the farm in this board book that features windows from which you can see the animals.

———. *Colores*. Susaeta, 2005.
This board book also features windows, from which you can see different colors.

Robleda, Margarita. *Dreams*. Santillana USA, 2004. Spanish: *Sueños*. Santillana USA, 2004.
> A child has pleasant dreams.

———. *Un grillo en mi cocina*. Sitesa, 1992.
> A child hears noises in the kitchen and goes to investigate and finds a cricket.

———. *Jugando con las vocales*. Santillana USA, 2006.
> A young child plays with her letters.

———. *Mis letras favoritas*. Ediciones Destino, 2003.
> Letters of the alphabet are introduced in rhyme.

———. *Ramón and His Mouse*. Santillana USA, 2004. Spanish: *Ramón y su ratón*. Santillana USA, 2004.
> Don Ramón has issues with a sneaky mouse.

———. *Una sorpresa para Ana Cristina*. Sitesa, 1992.
> Ana Cristina wants a cookie and finds a surprise waiting for her when she finally reaches the cookie jar.

Rondon, Javier. *Absent-Minded Toad*. Kane/Miller, 1994. Spanish: *El sapo distraído*. Sagebrush Education Resources, 1994.
> A toad forgets what he was going to buy at the market.

Rosa-Mendoza, Gladys. *The Alphabet / El alfabeto*. Me+mi, 2005.
> This board book features letters of the alphabet along with an illustration of an object starting with that letter.

———. *What Time Is It? / ¿Qué hora es?* Me+mi, 2005.
> A child learns the concept of time in this bilingual board book.

Roth, Susan L. *My Love for You / Mi amor por ti*. Dial, 2003.
> Two mice describe their love for each other in this bilingual board book.

Rubio, Gabriela. *¿Dónde estoy?* Ediciones Ekaré, 2007.
> In this illustrated book for little children, each animal finds itself on top of another animal of a different color until all of them find themselves piled up on a gray whale.

Ruiz-Flores, Lupe. *Lupita's Papalote / El papalote de Lupita*. Piñata Books, 2002.
> A young girl wants to fly a kite, but her family cannot afford to buy one, so her father helps her make a kite of her own.

Ryan, Pam Muñoz. *Hello, Ocean / Hola, Mar.* Charlesbridge, 2003.
    A child describes the ocean using the five senses.

————. *Mice and Beans.* Illustrated by Joe Cepeda. Scholastic, 2001.
    Spanish: *Arroz con frijoles y unos amables ratones.* Scholastic, 2001.
    Rosa María plans a birthday party for her special granddaughter
    and discovers that she had some help from some sneaky little mice.

Salas, Michele. *A Is for Alphabet / A de alfabeto.* Everest, 2003.
    Each letter is presented first in Spanish and then in English.

Salas-Porras, Pipina. *The Little Mouse / El ratoncito pequeño: A Nursery Rhyme in Spanish and English.* Cinco Puntos Press, 2001.
    What happens when hungry cats trick mice?

Salinas, Bobbi. *The Three Pigs / Los tres cerdos: Nacho, Tito, and Miguel.* Piñata Publications, 1998.
    With a big bad wolf named Jose and a trio of pigs named Tito,
    Nacho, and Miguel, a Mexican twist to the old fairy tale produces
    some lively antics.

Sánchez, Mireia. *Sobre la arena.* Combel, 2000.
    A family plays in the sand and makes sand castles.

Sempere, Vicky. *ABC.* Ediciones Ekaré, 1991.
    See what some of the animals do in this easy alphabet book.

————. *1, 2, 3: Un cuento para contar.* Ediciones Ekaré, 1995.
    Come to a birthday party with the animals in this easy counting
    book.

Shannon, David. *David Smells!* Scholastic, 2005. Spanish: *¡David huele!* Blue Sky Press, 2005.
    This board book features David, who has a stinky diaper.

Sirett, Dawn. *Baby's Busy World.* DK Publishing, 2005. Spanish: *Bebés atareados.* Molino, 2006.
    Simple text and photographs introduce colors, numbers, shapes,
    and first concepts, including helping out, busy vehicles, and
    playtime fun.

Sobrino, Javier. *Me gusta.* Kókinos, 2002.
    In this illustrated book, the children enjoy many things in daily
    life, including fresh air, the sun and moon, flowers, food, sleeping,
    games, planting things, and other activities.

Soto, Gary. *Chato's Kitchen.* Illustrated by Susan Guevara. Penguin Young Readers Group, 1995. Spanish: *Chato y su cena.* Sagebrush Education Resources, 1997.
> Chato and his pal Novio Boy are outsmarted by mice neighbors and their friend Chorizo.

———. *My Little Car / Mi carrito.* Putnam's, 2006.
> Teresa gets a shiny, new, pedal-powered lowrider car from Grandpa.

———. *The Old Man and His Door.* Sagebrush Education Resources, 1998. Spanish: *El viejo y su puerta.* Sagebrush Education Resources, 2003.
> An old man sets out for a party with a door on his back.

———. *Too Many Tamales.* Penguin Young Readers Group, 1996. Spanish: *Qué montón de tamales.* Tandem Library Books, 1996.
> María tries on her mother's wedding ring while helping make tamales for a Christmas family get-together, and panic ensues when she realizes the ring is missing.

Suárez, Maribel. *¿A qué sabe? El sentido del gusto.* Editorial Grijalbo, 1995.
> A cat shows what he likes and doesn't like to eat.

———. *Los contrarios.* Editorial Grijalbo, 1990.
> Animals introduce the concept of opposites.

———. *¿Cuántos son?* Editorial Grijalbo, 1992.
> Learn how to count in this Spanish book for children.

———. *Las formas.* Sagebrush Education Resources, 1999.
> Animals introduce the concept of shapes.

———. *The Letters / Las letras.* Editorial Grijalbo, 1990.
> An animal is presented for each letter of the alphabet.

Suen, Anastasia. *Baby Born.* Lee and Low Books, 2000. Spanish: *Recién nacido.* Lee and Low Books, 2000.
> This board book shows that babies grow with each season.

Tabor, Nancy. *Albertina Goes Up: An Alphabet Book / Albertina anda arriba: El abecedario.* Charlesbridge, 1992.
> Each page has a question that relates to a letter of the alphabet.

Tabor, Nancy Maria Grande. *A Taste of the Mexican Market / El gusto del mercado mexicano*. Charlesbridge, 1996.
> This book describes many of the different foods found at a Mexican market.

————. *We Are a Rainbow / Somos un arco iris*. Charlesbridge, 1997.
> Simple text and illustrations explore some of the similarities and differences that a child recognizes after moving to the United States from a Spanish-speaking country.

Tafolla, Carmen. *Baby Coyote and the Old Woman / El coyotito y la vieja: A Bilingual Story*. Wings Press, 2000.
> When the little old lady's trash blows away into the desert, the little coyote returns it to her doorstep.

————. *What Can You Do with a Rebozo?* Tricycle Press, 2008.
> Find out the many uses a child finds for her mother's *rebozo*, a traditional Mexican woven shawl.

Tello, Jerry. *Abuelo and the Three Bears / Abuelo y los tres osos*. Scholastic, 1997.
> An adaptation of a traditional tale.

Torres, Leyla. *Kite Festival*. Farrar, Straus, and Giroux, 2004. Spanish: *El festival de cometas*. Farrar, Straus, and Giroux, 2004.
> While on a Sunday outing, Fernando and his family encounter a kite festival and decide to create a kite from scrap materials so that they can join in.

————. *Liliana's Grandmothers / Las abuelas de Liliana*. Farrar, Straus, and Giroux, 1998.
> Liliana has two grandmothers, one in the United States and one in South America.

Urdaneta, Josefina. *Busca que te busca*. Playco Editores, 2000.
> A duck searches for her rubber boots.

Vargo, Sharon. *Señor Felipe's Alphabet Adventure: El alfabeto español*. Millbrook Press, 2000.
> Señor Felipe is given the mission to photograph things that begin with each letter of the Spanish alphabet.

Velasquez, Eric. *Grandma's Records*. Walker, 2001. Spanish: *Los discos de mi abuela*. Lectorum Publications, 2002.
> The author describes his boyhood summers spent at his grandmother's apartment in Spanish Harlem, where she introduced him to the sounds and steps of the merengue and the conga, and told him stories of Puerto Rico.

Villaseñor, Victor. *Mother Fox and the Coyote / Mamá Zorra y Don Coyote*. Piñata Books, 2004.
> Mother Fox convinces Don Coyote that the moon's reflection is really a giant cheese.

———. *The Stranger and the Red Rooster / El forastero y el gallo rojo*. Piñata Books, 2006.
> A stranger has everyone on alert, and why does he have a red rooster?

Walsh, Ellen Stoll. *Mouse Count*. Harcourt Children's Books, 1995. Spanish: *Cuenta ratones*. Fondo de Cultura Económica, 2003.
> It's time to count with mice.

Weeks, Sarah. *Counting Ovejas*. Atheneum Books for Young Readers, 2006.
> A child tries to remove the sheep that appear in his room as he tries to fall asleep.

Wheeler, Lisa. *Te amo, Bebé, Little One*. Little, Brown, 2004.
> A mother repeats how much she loves her baby.

Wildsmith, Brian. *Animal Colors / Los colores de los animales*. Star Bright Books, 2005.
> This board book shows colorful animals in their natural settings.

Wood, Audrey. *Piggies / Cerditos: Lap-Sized Board Book*. Harcourt, 2008.
> Ten little piggies dance along a child's fingers and toes.

Zepeda, Gwendolyn. *Growing Up with Tamales / Los tamales de Ana*. Piñata Books, 2008.
> Ana can hardly wait to be old enough to have more responsibility with the traditional Christmas tamales.

INDEX OF TITLES AND FIRST LINES

Note: Entries enclosed in quotation marks are first lines. English and Spanish articles are included in alphabetization.

INDEX OF CRAFT IDEAS

You may also be interested in

The Pura Belpré Awards: In this inaugural reference covering the first ten years of the Pura Belpré Awards, editor Rose Zertuche Treviño, in conjunction with ALSC and REFORMA, shares the celebration with all librarians who love great kids' books and cultural diversity. This helpful reference also includes a bonus DVD and special color section!

¡Bienvenidos! ¡Welcome!: To create a comprehensive marketing and outreach strategy that will attract diverse Latino audiences, Byrd suggests ways to gain knowledge of your Latino community through interviews, surveys, and an advisory council. You will also learn what collections and programs have been successful in other libraries with a large base of Spanish-language users, as well as tried-and-true methods to gain knowledge about your local Latino community.

Flannelboard Stories for Infants and Toddlers, Bilingual Edition: With the growth of Latino populations in the United States, libraries must address the challenges of serving an increasing customer base of Spanish speakers, many of whom have infant children. This Spanish-English bilingual guide features thirty-three original stories, chants, songs, and nursery rhyme adaptations for the youngest library customers—between 12 and 30 months old.

25 Latino Craft Projects: Libraries can serve as a nucleus where people with different backgrounds and traditions can come together and learn from each other. While Latinos are the fastest growing ethnic group in the United States, this book acts as a powerful tool for reaching out to everyone—Latinos and non-Latinos alike. Use Borrego and Pavon's tips on developing and publicizing unique cultural programs to make a lasting impression on your community.

Check out these and other great titles at www.alastore.ala.org!